POWER FOOD

over **100 nourishing** recipes
to **recharge, revitalize**
& rejuvenate

Dedicated, in loving memory, to our dear friend and colleague Rachel Harper

This edition published by Parragon Books Ltd in 2016 and distributed by

Parragon Inc.
440 Park Avenue South, 13th Floor
New York, NY 10016
www.parragon.com/lovefood

LOVE FOOD is an imprint of Parragon Books Ltd

ISBN 978-1-4748-1755-4

Printed in China

Introduction by Fiona Hunter
New recipes by Joy Skipper
New photography by Al Richardson
Home economy and food styling by Laurie Perry
Project editor Emma Clegg
Production by Fiona Rhys-Griffith
Designed by Beth Kalynka

Notes for the Reader
This book uses standard kitchen measuring spoons and cups. All spoon and cup measurements are level unless otherwise indicated. Unless otherwise stated, milk is assumed to be whole, eggs are large, individual vegetables are medium, and pepper is freshly ground black pepper. A pinch of salt is calculated as $\frac{1}{16}$ of a teaspoon. Unless otherwise stated, all root vegetables should be peeled prior to using.

The times given are an approximate guide only. Preparation times differ according to the techniques used by different people, and the cooking times may also vary from those given.

Please note that any ingredients stated as being optional are not included in the nutritional values provided. The nutritional values given are approximate and provided as a guideline only, they do not account for individual cooks, scales, and portion sizes. The nutritional values provided are per serving or per item.

POWER
into Health

If you want to live a long and healthy life, eating a balanced diet and staying active are two of the most important things you can do. The former can reduce the risk of a long list of medical problems, including heart disease, stroke, some types of cancer, cataracts, and dementia. The right diet can also help strengthen your immune system. But what exactly is a healthy, balanced diet?

The rules are simple: eat less saturated and trans fat, salt, sugar, and processed foods and more fruit and vegetables, whole grains, unrefined fiber-rich carbs, and healthy fats. But how do we translate these rules into tasty, balanced meals that the whole family will enjoy?

That's where this book can help. Here, you'll find over 100 recipes, each one packed with goodness and flavor. The recipes focus on fresh, minimally processed ingredients—foods that are naturally rich in vitamins, minerals, essential fatty acids, and disease-fighting phytochemicals, foods that pack a real punch when it comes to nutrition.

Whether you want a quick-and-easy lunch or a power breakfast to keep you going all morning, you'll find plenty of inspiration. There are family favorites, such as Flatbread Pizza with Zucchini Ribbons and Moroccan Lamb Burgers, as well as healthy treats, such as Chocolate & Brazil Nut Bars and Zucchini Loaf Cake. All the recipes have a complete nutritional breakdown with information on calories, fat, saturated fat, fiber, protein, carbohydrate, sugar, salt, and dietary fiber.

Integrating fresh fruit and vegetables (right) and whole grains, such as quinoa, buckwheat, and bulgur wheat (below), into your diet will help you power up your day.

Healthy-Eating Essentials

One of the key ingredients in a healthy diet is balance. To help you get the right balance, nutritionists divide foods into five food groups. To be sure you get all the nutrients your body needs, you should eat some food from each of the first four food groups each day:

- Starchy carbohydrates, such as bread, pasta, and potatoes
- Fruit and vegetables
- Milk and other dairy products
- Protein-rich foods, such as meat, fish, and dried beans and other legumes
- Foods and beverages containing fat and sugar

Bread, cereals and grains, pasta, rice, noodles, and potatoes

Food in this group provides energy and dietary fiber along with a range of vitamins, minerals, and small amounts of protein. Choosing whole-grain options, such as whole wheat bread, brown rice, and unrefined cereals, will help to keep your digestive system and heart healthy.

Fruit and vegetables

Most of us know we need to eat plenty of fruit and vegetables a day. However, it is also important to eat a variety.

Above: Fresh fruits are low in calories and fat and packed with health-boosting nutrients, such as vitamins, minerals, antioxidants, and phytonutrients.

Fruit and vegetables in different colors contain different vitamins, minerals, and phytochemicals, which help to keep you healthy in different ways. Think of the colors in a rainbow and aim to eat fruit and vegetables from each of these color bands over the course of a week.

Milk, yogurt, and cheese

Foods in this group are an important source of calcium, essential for maintaining strong, healthy bones. They also provide

Below: Dairy products are rich in calcium and are easily digested and absorbed by the body.

protein, vitamins A, D, and B2. Getting enough calcium while your bones are still growing will help to reduce the risk of osteoporosis later in life, but calcium is important even when your bones have finished growing. If you can, choose reduced- and low-fat alternatives, such as skim and low-fat milk.

Meat, fish, eggs, dried beans and other legumes, nuts, and seeds

Foods in this group provide protein that is essential for growth and the repair of cells. They also provide important vitamins and minerals. Choose lean cuts of meat and keep servings modest. Try to eat at least two servings of fish a week, making one of them an oil-rich variety, such as salmon, mackerel, or fresh tuna. Oil-rich fish are rich in omega-3 fatty acids, which can help reduce the risk of heart disease and strokes.

Foods containing sugar and fat

Foods in this group include butter, margarine, low-fat spreads, salad dressings, mayonnaise, potato chips, cream, cookies, pastries, cakes and other desserts, soft drinks, chocolate, and confectionery. Most of us enjoy eating foods from this group, and the good news is that you don't need to deny yourself— providing you eat them in moderation, as part of a balanced diet. It is possible to choose healthier options, too, so whenever possible choose reduced fat and/or sugar options.

Energy & Health

When we talk about energy, we are generally referring to the energy we require to do everyday things—working, shopping, and domestic chores as well as socializing, exercising, looking after the family, and enjoying life. However, energy can also refer to the amount of energy, or the number of calories, that a food provides. Both types of energy are important for our vitality and well-being. An unhealthy diet—perhaps skipping meals and not drinking enough water—can sap your energy levels, leaving you feeling lethargic and unmotivated.

To keep your energy levels buoyant, you need to eat little and often, choosing healthy, balanced meals and snacks. Focus on unrefined, fiber-rich carbohydrates, which will be broken down into sugars more slowly, help keep blood sugar levels stable, help keep hunger pangs at bay, and prevent energy levels from crashing.

A healthy diet should also provide you with the right amount of energy (calories) to maintain a healthy body weight. Being overweight increases the risk of a number of health problems, including heart disease, diabetes, high blood pressure, stroke, infertility, and some types of cancer.

Above: Vegetables rich in calcium include lettuce, broccoli, kale, green beans, fennel, and asparagus.

Our weight is determined by the balance between the energy (calories) we consume from food and beverages, and the energy (calories) we burn. The body burns calories every day as it pumps blood around the body, breathes, and regulates temperature, but you can also burn calories and use energy by being active and exercising.

If the calories you take in and calories you use are in balance, then your weight stays stable, but if you take in more calories than you burn, then the extra calories are stored as fat. Unfortunately, it only takes a small imbalance between the calories consumed and the calories used to create a weight problem.

Below: Nuts, avocados, and vegetable oils supply us with the healthy unsaturated fats that are vital to keep the body healthy.

The amount of energy an individual needs to consume is determined by many factors, including age, sex, and genetics. An average woman needs about 2,000 calories a day and an average man about 2,500. The recipes in this book are accompanied by a nutritional breakdown that includes the number of calories per serving, so you can use this to help you determine how many calories you are eating each day. Use the table below as a guide to help you plan your menus.

	Men	Women
Calories	2,500	2,000
Total fat (g)	Less than 80	Less than 65
Saturated fat	Less than 25	Less than 20
Protein (g)	55	45
Carbohydrate	375	300
Total sugars	Less than 120	Less than 90
Fiber (g)	30g	25g
Sodium (mg)	Less than 2,400	Less than 2,400

Dawn to Dusk Healthy Eating

Breakfast is said to be the most important meal of the day, and there is much truth in this. Put simply, after 10–12 hours without food, your body needs fuel. The first meal of the day is only part of the story, but if you have a wholesome nutritious breakfast, such as the Layered Power Smoothie Bowl on page 18 or the Avocado Toasts on page 20, you'll reap the benefits for the rest of the day.

Studies show that what you eat at breakfast can affect your mood and your physical and mental performance during the morning as well as your long-term health. If you can't face the idea of eating much when you first get up, try taking the easily portable Superfood Breakfast Bars on page 26 or the Rise & Shine Muffins on page 34 to work.

Eating little and often is the best way to keep blood sugar levels stable, the mind focused, and the body healthy. So don't skip lunch. Making a healthy, nutritious lunch doesn't have to take a lot of time or effort—you can use recipes, such as Quinoa Salad in a Jar on page 72 and the Rainbow Power Rolls on page 82, both easy to prepare the night before.

Above: Naturally sweet vegetables, such as sweet potato, bell peppers, onions, sweet corn, and carrots add a healthy sweetness to the meals you prepare.

Make sure your body gets all the vitamins and minerals it needs by focusing on foods that are nutrient-rich and avoiding highly refined and processed foods that provide loads of saturated fat, sugar, and calories. This is why it's important to cook meals from scratch as much as possible instead of relying on prepared meals and convenience foods.

Eating healthily doesn't have to be difficult, but it does mean some planning. Taking a few minutes to plan your menu for the week ahead will help you to make sure that your diet is varied and balanced. Having a plan also means you won't have to think about it during the week when you are tired.

Remember that eating healthily is important to keep us feeling fresh, healthy, and energized, but it can also be plenty of fun, and eating good food is one of the great pleasures in life. So get going and enjoy all the sources of power within these pages to the max.

Left: Potassium is essential for the heart to maintain strong muscles, for nerve conduction, and to reduce the incidence of strokes. Potassium-rich foods include tomatoes, apricots, bananas, zucchini, and various types of beans.

You should never skip breakfast, say the health experts. Well, once you've taken a look at some of the bold, power-into-your-day delights in this chapter—from a Morning Power Smoothie Bowl to Spinach & Nutmeg Baked Eggs, to Avocado Toasts and Spicy Black Bean & Corn Scramble—you'll likely to be stocking up on some key power ingredients so that breakfast becomes a normal part of your daily menu.

JUMP-START

Morning Power Smoothie Bowl

Serves: 1 | Prep: 10 minutes, plus chilling | Cook: none

Per serving: 654 CAL | 34.4G FAT | 13.8G SAT FAT | 86.9G CARBS | 51.1G SUGAR | 19.5G FIBER | 11.1G PROTEIN | 40MG SODIUM

Here's a great way to increase your nutrient intake, with plenty of colorful fruits to provide antioxidants and healthy fats from nuts and seeds.

Ingredients

⅛ cup hulled strawberries

⅛ cup blackberries

⅛ cup raspberries

1 banana, peeled

⅔ cup hemp milk

1 tablespoon coconut oil

1 tablespoon ground almonds (almond meal)

1 kiwi, peeled and sliced

2 teaspoons chia seeds

1 small mango, pitted, peeled, and chopped

1 tablespoon chopped walnuts

2 teaspoons toasted sesame seeds

1. Put the strawberries, blackberries, raspberries, half the banana, the hemp milk, coconut oil, and ground almonds into a blender and blend until smooth.

2. Pour into a bowl and place the remaining ingredients on top to serve.

Why Not Try?

You can add ground nuts or seeds to the fruit layers to thicken them and add nutrients—try some ground golden flaxseed meal in the mango for extra essential fats and fiber.

Layered Power Smoothie Bowl

Serves: 2 | Prep: 1–15 minutes | Cook: none

Per serving: 303 CAL | 6.4G FAT | 1.1G SAT FAT | 61.3G CARBS | 44.2 SUGAR | 7.1G FIBER | 6.4G PROTEIN | TRACE SODIUM

This colorful smoothie not only looks stunning, but the combination of flavors is delicious. Rich in antioxidants from the fruits, with additional protein from the chlorella powder, almonds, and sesame seeds, it is a great breakfast.

Ingredients

1 large mango, pitted, peeled, and chopped

2 kiwis, peeled and chopped

⅛ teaspoon chlorella powder

3 cups peeled watermelon chunks (with the seeds for vitamin E)

1 tablespoon ground almonds (almond meal)

1 teaspoon sesame seeds

2 tablespoons granola

large pinch of ground cinnamon

1. Put the mango into a small blender and process until smooth. Divide between two glass bowls. Rinse the blender.

2. Put the kiwi and chlorella powder into the blender and process until smooth. Spoon the puree over the mango in the bowls. Rinse the blender.

3. Put the watermelon into the blender and process until smooth. Add the ground almonds and sesame seeds and process briefly to combine. Spoon the watermelon puree over the kiwi mixture.

4. Sprinkle with the granola and ground cinnamon and serve.

Avocado Toasts

Serves: 4 | Prep: 10 minutes | Cook: 10 minutes

Per serving : 896 CAL | 65.5G FAT | 8.6G SAT FAT | 67.8G CARBS | 5.2G SUGAR | 24G FIBER | 22.5G PROTEIN | 920MG SODIUM

Avocado is rich in omega-3 fats, the healthy fats we all need to keep our cells and brains functioning well. This recipe makes a quick-and-simple, yet nutritious, breakfast—topped with healthy spiced nuts and seeds.

Ingredients

8 slices multigrain bread

¼ cup tahini

4 large avocados, peeled, pitted, and sliced

Hazelnut Topping

1 cup hazelnuts

⅓ cup sesame seeds

2 tablespoons cumin seeds

2 tablespoons coriander seeds

2 teaspoons pepper

1 teaspoon sea salt

1. To make the hazelnut topping, preheat the oven to 350°F.

2. Spread the hazelnuts over a baking sheet and bake in the preheated oven for 3–4 minutes. Rub them in a clean dish towel to remove the skins.

3. Put the hazelnuts into a food processor and process until coarsely chopped.

4. Dry-fry the sesame seeds in a skillet over medium heat for 1–2 minutes, until golden. Put the sesame seeds and hazelnuts into a bowl.

5. Add the cumin seeds and coriander seeds to the pan and dry-fry for 1–2 minutes, then crush in a mortar and pestle. Add the spices, pepper, and salt to the nuts and seeds and mix well together.

6. Toast the bread and spread each slice with tahini.

7. Top each toast with half an avocado, mashing it lightly with a fork, then sprinkle with the hazelnut topping to serve.

Why Not Try?

Roasted cherry tomatoes with cumin seeds and a little olive oil, and serve them on the avocado, sprinkled with feta cheese and black pepper.

Mango

The mango is a nutritional superstar among fruits, being rich in antioxidants and vitamins C and E. Its orange flesh contains more antioxidant beta-carotene than most other fruits, which can protect against some cancers and heart disease. The medium—low glycemic index of mangoes also means that they help regulate blood sugar levels.

Acai Knockout

Serves: 1 | Prep: 10 minutes | Cook: none

Per serving : 129 CAL | 6G FAT | 2.2G SAT FAT | 16.7G CARBS | 12.1G SUGAR | 2.8G FIBER | 3.8G PROTEIN | 120MG SODIUM

This power smoothie is an effective energy booster—it's perfect for breakfast, as an afternoon pick-me-up, or whenever you need an energy recharge.

Ingredients
2¾ cups spinach
2 teaspoons acai powder
2 teaspoons manuka honey
pinch of ground cinnamon
1 cup almond milk
crushed ice, to serve

1. Put the spinach, acai powder, honey, and cinnamon into a blender.

2. Pour in the almond milk and blend until smooth and creamy.

3. Stir well, pour it over the crushed ice, and serve immediately.

Almond Milk

As well as offering a nondairy option, almond milk is overflowing with health benefits: it helps with weight management, keeping your heart healthy, your skin glowing, and contributing to muscle strength and healthy digestion.

Superfood Breakfast Bars

Makes: 12 | Prep: 10 minutes | Cook: 20–25 minutes

Per serving : 245 CAL | 15.4G FAT | 9.5G SAT FAT | 24.7G CARBS | 9.5G SUGAR | 3G FIBER | 3.5G PROTEIN | TRACE SODIUM

These nutrient-dense breakfast bars will sustain you through the morning. Filled with oats, nuts, and blueberries, they are a delicious way to start your day. Blackstrap molasses, available at most health food stores, is rich in B vitamins.

Ingredients

2 teaspoons butter, for greasing

⅓ cup coconut oil

¼ cup blackstrap molasses

1½ tablespoons packed dark brown sugar

1 tablespoon agave syrup

2⅔ cups rolled oats

½ cup coarsely chopped pecans

½ cup cacao nibs

⅓ cup blueberries

1. Preheat the oven to 350°F. Grease a 7-inch square cake pan.

2. Put the coconut oil, molasses, sugar, and agave syrup into a large saucepan and heat until melted. Stir until the sugar has dissolved, then remove from the heat.

3. Stir in the remaining ingredients and mix them well together.

4. Pour into the prepared pan and level the top.

5. Bake in the preheated oven for 18–20 minutes, then let cool in the pan for 5 minutes before cutting into squares.

6. Let cool in the pan completely.

7. Store in an airtight container for up to five days.

Coconut Your Brain

Coconut oil is full of fatty acids,
but the oil has powerful medicinal
properties, including improved brain
function, increased energy, and an
ability to fight infection.

Sweet Potato & Kale Breakfast Bowl

Serves: 2 | Prep: 5 minutes | Cook: 10 minutes

Per serving : 571 CAL | 31.8G FAT | 7.9G SAT FAT | 56.7G CARBS | 11.9G SUGAR | 13.1G FIBER | 22.7G PROTEIN | 200MG SODIUM

This is a filling breakfast bowl that is full of goodness. Colorful steamed vegetables are tossed with warming spices and topped with a poached egg and a sprinkling of nuts for extra protein.

Ingredients

3 sweet potatoes, peeled and cut into chunks

3 cups chopped kale

2 eggs

2 teaspoons coconut oil

1 teaspoon cumin seeds

1 teaspoon mustard seeds

1 teaspoon pepper

½ teaspoon ground turmeric

¼ cup chopped walnuts

3 tablespoons blanched almonds, chopped

3 tablespoons pumpkin seeds

1. Put the sweet potatoes into a steamer and cook for 5–6 minutes, until tender. Add the kale to the steamer for the last 2 minutes of cooking.

2. Meanwhile, bring a small saucepan of water to a boil, break the eggs into a cup, one at a time, add to the pan, and poach for 4–5 minutes.

3. Heat the oil in a large skillet or wok and add the cumin seeds, mustard seeds, pepper, and turmeric. Cook until the mustard seeds begin to "pop," then add the steamed vegetables and toss.

4. Divide the spiced vegetables between two warm bowls and top each one with a poached egg.

5. Sprinkle each serving with walnuts, almonds, and pumpkin seeds and serve immediately.

Apple & Seed Muesli

Serves: 10 | Prep: 15–20 minutes | Cook: 4–5 minutes

Per serving : 324.0 CAL | 8.3G FAT | 1.4G SAT FAT | 45.5G CARBS | 15.1G SUGAR | 5.7G FIBER | 9G PROTEIN | TRACE SODIUM

Nutty and fruity, this muesli combination provides an undeniably healthy start to the day. Serve with milk or yogurt.

Ingredients

½ cup sunflower seeds

⅓ cup pumpkin seeds

¾ cup coarsely chopped hazelnuts

3 cups buckwheat flakes

3 cups rice flakes

¾ cup millet flakes

1⅓ cups coarsely chopped dried apple

¾ cup coarsely chopped dried pitted dates

1. Heat a nonstick skillet over medium heat. Add the seeds and hazelnuts and lightly toast, shaking the pan frequently, for 4 minutes, or until golden brown. Transfer to a large bowl and let cool.

2. Add the flakes, apple, and dates to the bowl and mix thoroughly until combined. Store the muesli in an airtight jar or container.

Spinach & Nutmeg Baked Eggs

Serves: 4 | Prep: 20 minutes, plus chilling | Cook: 20–30 minutes

Per serving : 235 CAL | 16.5G FAT | 4.2G SAT FAT | 7.5G CARBS | 1.6G SUGAR | 1.1G FIBER | 14.2G PROTEIN | 160MG SODIUM

Nutrient-rich fresh spinach adds delicious flavor and color to this popular egg dish, lightly seasoned with ground nutmeg. Serve with whole-grain bread for a wholesome breakfast or brunch.

Ingredients

1 tablespoon olive oil, for frying, plus extra for brushing

4 shallots, finely chopped

3 garlic cloves, sliced

3½ cups baby spinach

8 eggs

½ teaspoon ground nutmeg

salt and pepper, to taste (optional)

1. Preheat the oven to 350°F. Lightly brush the insides of four 1-cup ramekins (individual ceramic dishes) with olive oil.

2. Heat the olive oil in a skillet. Once hot, add the shallots and garlic and sauté over medium heat for 3–4 minutes, or until soft. Add the baby spinach and stir for 2–3 minutes, or until just wilted. Season with salt and pepper, if using.

3. Spoon the spinach mixture into the bottom of the prepared ramekins and crack two eggs into each. Sprinkle with the nutmeg and place the ramekins in a roasting pan. Fill the roasting pan with boiling water until the water reaches halfway up the ramekins—this will create a steamy environment for the eggs so they do not dry out.

4. Carefully transfer the roasting pan to the preheated oven for 15–20 minutes. Let the ramekins cool slightly, then serve immediately.

Fruity Insides

If you don't have raspberries
available, blueberries or halved
strawberries taste just as good.

Rise & Shine Muffins

Makes: 12 | Prep: 15 minutes | Cook: 25 minutes

Per serving : 277 CAL | 12.1G FAT | 8.7G SAT FAT | 37.7G CARBS | 13.3G SUGAR | 3.9G FIBER | 5.9G PROTEIN | 80MG SODIUM

These nutrient-packed muffins are perfect for a breakfast or brunch, or even to take on a picnic, because they are easy to pack for traveling. You can also make them in advance, freeze separately, then take out the number you need and thaw.

Ingredients

1 cup all-purpose white flour

⅔ cup whole wheat flour

2 teaspoons baking powder

½ teaspoon ground cinnamon

⅓ cup packed light brown sugar

1¼ cups granola

½ cup rolled oats

2 bananas, peeled and mashed

1 cup Greek-style yogurt

½ cup milk

½ cup coconut oil, melted

1⅔ cups raspberries

1 tablespoon pumpkin seeds

1. Preheat the oven to 400°F. Line the sections in a 12-cup muffin pan with 4½-inch squares of parchment paper.

2. Put the white flour, whole wheat flour, baking powder, cinnamon, sugar, granola, and oats into a large bowl.

3. In a separate bowl, mix together the bananas, yogurt, milk, and coconut oil.

4. Pour the wet ingredients into the dry ingredients and lightly mix. Set aside 12 raspberries, then add the remaining raspberries and mix again; do not overmix—some flour should still be showing.

5. Divide the batter among the 12 paper liners, then top each muffin with a raspberry and sprinkle with the pumpkin seeds.

6. Bake in the preheated oven for 25 minutes, until golden and risen. Let cool in the pan for 5 minutes, then turn out onto a wire rack and let cool completely.

Buckwheat Breakfast Bowl

Serves: 4 | Prep: 20–25 minutes, plus 36 hours sprouting | Cook: none

Per serving : 452 CAL | 22.4G FAT | 17.5G SAT FAT | 58G CARBS | 22.8G SUGAR | 9.8G FIBER | 10.1G PROTEIN | 40MG SODIUM

Buckwheat has been eaten since Paleolithic times. It makes a tasty cereal and, being a source of complex carbohydrates, provides an excellent boost of energy.

Ingredients

¾ cups plus 2 tablespoons buckwheat

2 cups cold water, preferably filtered

1¾ cups coconut yogurt

grated zest and juice of 1 orange

3 tablespoons goji berries

¾ cup raspberries

1 Granny Smith apple, cored and diced

1 tablespoon pumpkin seeds

2 passion fruit, pulp only

2 teaspoons ground cinnamon

½ teaspoon ground turmeric

seeds of 1 pomegranate

2 tablespoons agave syrup

1. Rinse the buckwheat three times in fresh water to clean the groats. Place in a bowl with the cold water and soak for 20 minutes.

2. Drain and rinse the buckwheat, then let stand at room temperature—in either a sprouting tray or a strainer with a bowl beneath—for 36 hours. Rinse the buckwheat if the groats look sticky, then again before using.

3. Rinse, drain, and divide the buckwheat among four bowls. Divide the yogurt among the bowls, sprinkle with the remaining ingredients, and serve.

Buck Up

This recipe uses buckwheat that has been sprouted for 36 hours; it can be done in less time, but a longer time gives optimum nutrition.

Fruity Puffed Quinoa

Serves: 1 | Prep: 5 minutes, plus standing | Cook: none

Per serving : 360 CAL | 5.3G FAT | 0.8G SAT FAT | 78.1G CARBS | 46.3G SUGAR | 8.9G FIBER | 6.6G PROTEIN | TRACE SODIUM

Quinoa puffs are a healthy alternative to regular breakfast cereal. Here, apple juice is used to moisten the puffs instead of the more commonly used milk. It makes a particularly refreshing start to the day and is a good solution if you don't like milk on your cereal.

Ingredients

⅓ cup puffed quinoa

½ cup apple juice

1 small banana, thinly sliced

½ crisp, red-skinned apple, sliced into thin wedges

2 teaspoons pumpkin seeds

honey, for drizzling

Greek-style yogurt, to serve (optional)

1. Put the puffed quinoa into a serving bowl. Stir in the apple juice, making sure the puffs are submerged. Let stand for a few minutes.

2. Arrange the banana slices and apple wedges on top of the quinoa.

3. Sprinkle with the pumpkin seeds and drizzle with a little honey. Serve immediately with yogurt, if using.

Spicy Black Bean & Corn Scramble

Serves: 2 | Prep: 10 minutes, plus 2 hours cooling | Cook: 20 minutes

Per serving : 427 CAL | 19.9G FAT | 4G SAT FAT | 43.2G CARBS | 2.4G SUGAR | 3.9G FIBER | 19G PROTEIN | 1,080MG SODIUM

A Mexican-inspired version of scrambled eggs on toast, using Italian-style polenta instead of bread, this dish makes a great weekend breakfast or brunch.

Ingredients

½ cup fine yellow cornmeal

1 teaspoon low-sodium vegetable bouillon powder

1 tablespoon nutritional yeast flakes

⅛ teaspoon sea salt

1 tablespoon extra virgin canola oil, plus 1 teaspoon for brushing

¼ cup finely chopped red onion

3 tablespoons finely chopped red bell pepper

1 small garlic clove, crushed

3 tablespoons corn kernels, cooked

3 tablespoons black beans, cooked and rinsed

dash of sugar-free chili sauce

4 eggs, beaten

1. Line a 6-inch square shallow dish or baking pan with parchment paper.

2. Make the polenta at least 2 hours before you want to toast it. Put the cornmeal into a small bowl. Bring 1½ cups of water to a boil in a saucepan with the vegetable bouillon powder and, when it is boiling rapidly, gradually pour in the cornmeal, stirring all the time. Continue cooking and stirring over high heat for 3 minutes, until it thickens. Turn the heat down, stir in the yeast and salt, and simmer, stirring, until you have a thick paste.

3. Spoon the cornmeal mixture into the prepared dish or pan. Cover with plastic wrap or aluminum foil and place in the refrigerator for 2 hours or until firm. Cut into four triangles.

4. Add half of the oil to a small skillet and put over medium heat. Cook the onion and bell pepper for 7 minutes, or until soft. Stir in the garlic, corn, beans, and chili sauce and cook for an additional minute. Set aside and keep warm.

5. Preheat a ridged grill pan or the broiler to medium. Brush the polenta triangles with the oil and grill or broil until turning golden and flecked dark brown. Grill or broil the other side.

6. In a separate, small skillet, add the remaining oil and put over medium heat. Add the eggs and cook, stirring with a spatula or wooden spoon from time to time until lightly scrambled. Lightly stir the bean mixture into the eggs and serve with the toasted polenta.

Buckwheat

Buckwheat, contrary to its name, contains no wheat, is gluten-free, and has a low glycaemic index. It lowers the risk of developing high cholesterol and high blood pressure and it is rich in flavonoids, antioxidants that protect against disease. Buckwheat also cleans and strengthens intestines, improves appetite, and is an excellent source of easily digestible protein.

Coconut Power Bowl

Serves: 4 | Prep: 20 minutes | Cook: 15 minutes

Per serving: 746 CAL | 43.1G FAT | 26G SAT FAT | 84.7G CARBS | 31.3G SUGAR | 11.3G FIBER | 11.8G PROTEIN | 40MG SODIUM

This recipe uses a delicious homemade quinoa granola, which is richer in protein and lower in sugar than most store-bought granolas. It's served on a creamy coconut-and-banana "porridge" that includes plenty of omega-3 fats from the walnuts and pecans, plus antioxidants from the raspberries and cranberries.

Ingredients

½ cup coconut oil

1 tablespoon honey

2 tablespoons packed dark brown sugar

1 cup quinoa flakes

1⅔ cups rolled oats

3 tablespoons dry unsweeten coconut

½ teaspoon ground cinnamon

1 tablespoon dried cranberries

1 tablespoon chopped pecans

2 bananas, peeled and chopped

½ cup walnuts

1 cup coconut milk

1 teaspoon ground cinnamon

¾ cup raspberries

small handful of mint leaves

2 tablespoons maple syrup

1. Preheat the oven to 350°F. Put the coconut oil, honey, and sugar into a saucepan over low heat and heat, stirring, until the sugar has dissolved.

2. Remove from the heat and stir in the quinoa flakes, ⅔ cup of the oats, 2 tablespoons of the dry coconut, the cinnamon, cranberries, and pecans. Mix well to combine.

3. Spread the mixture over a baking sheet and bake in the preheated oven for 15 minutes, stirring halfway through the cooking time.

4. Remove from the oven, spoon into a bowl, and let cool.

5. Meanwhile, put the bananas, the remaining oats, the walnuts, and coconut milk into a food processor and process until almost smooth.

6. Pour into four bowls and add the granola. Top with the cinnamon, raspberries, mint, the remaining dry coconut, and a drizzle of maple syrup.

Greek-Style Yogurt with Toasted Seeds

Serves: 2 | Prep: 5 minutes | Cook: 3 minutes

Per serving : 152 CAL | 8.9G FAT | 4.G SAT FAT | 7.7G CARBS | 4.1G SUGAR | 2.7G FIBER | 11.1G PROTEIN | 40MG SODIUM

Toasting the seeds in this recipe enhances their flavor, so they contrast wonderfully with the smooth, creamy yogurt.

Ingredients

2 teaspoons flaxseed

2 teaspoons pumpkin seeds

2 teaspoons chia seeds

1 cup Greek-style plain yogurt

grated zest of 1 small orange, plus 1 teaspoon juice

1. Put a small skillet over medium heat. When it is hot, add the seeds. Toast, stirring constantly with a wooden spoon, for 3 minutes, or until they begin to turn brown and release a nutty aroma. Transfer them to a plate and let cool.

2. Spoon the yogurt into two glass jars or serving bowls, then sprinkle the seeds on top, followed by the orange zest. Sprinkle with the orange juice and serve immediately.

Zucchini Hash Browns with Eggs & Salmon

Serves: 2 | Prep: 30 minutes | Cook: 18 minutes

Per serving: 538 CAL | 41.6G FAT | 16G SAT FAT | 10.1G CARBS | 4.5G SUGAR | 2.1G FIBER | 31.2G PROTEIN | 1,800G SODIUM

Zucchini make a great substitute for potatoes in these tasty hash browns; their subtle, creamy flavor complements the luxurious egg and salmon perfectly.

Ingredients

3 extra-large eggs

1 tablespoon heavy cream

2 teaspoons finely snipped fresh chives

1 tablespoon butter

sea salt and pepper, to taste (optional)

2 large slices of smoked salmon, to serve

Hash Browns

1½ zucchini, shredded (about 2⅔ cups prepared)

2 teaspoons quinoa flour

¼ cup grated Parmesan cheese

1 extra-large egg yolk

1 tablespoon heavy cream

1 tablespoon vegetable oil

1. Preheat the oven to 225°F. To make the hash browns, lay a clean dish towel on a work surface and pile the zucchini in the center. Holding the dish towel over the sink, gather the sides together and twist them tightly until all the liquid from the zucchini has run out.

2. Put the zucchini, flour, Parmesan, egg yolk, and cream into a bowl and mix well. Roll the mixture into two balls and flatten them with the palms of your hands to make thick patties.

3. Heat the oil in a small skillet over medium–low heat. Cook the hash browns for 5–8 minutes on each side, until golden brown. Remove, transfer to a baking sheet, and put into the oven to keep warm.

4. To make the scrambled eggs, crack the eggs into a bowl, add the cream and chives, and season with salt and pepper, if using. Beat with a fork.

5. Wipe the skillet clean with paper towels, then melt the butter in the pan over low heat. Pour in the egg mixture and cook, stirring, for 5–6 minutes, or until the eggs are just set.

6. Put the hash browns on two warm plates. Spoon the scrambled eggs over them, then top with the salmon. Grind over some black pepper, if using, and serve immediately.

Boston
Baked Beans

Serves: 4 | Prep: 10 minutes | Cook: 40 minutes

Per serving : 573 CAL | 25.5G FAT | 4G SAT FAT | 56.4G CARBS | 14.8G SUGAR | 14.6G FIBER | 27.5G PROTEIN | 320MG SODIUM

Making your own baked beans is delightfully simple, as well as being tasty and nutritious. You can add your favorite ingredients, really making the recipe your own. Cooked tomatoes are rich in lycopene, a powerful antioxidant. Topped with a poached egg, these beans make a protein-rich breakfast.

Ingredients

2 ripe tomatoes
1 tablespoon olive oil
1 tablespoon sesame seeds
1 tablespoon pumpkin seeds
1 tablespoon sunflower seeds
1¾ cups roasted red peppers
2–3 tablespoons vegetable broth
1 (28-ounce) can navy beans, drained
⅓ cup raisins
½ cup slivered almonds
small handful of fresh cilantro
4 slices sourdough bread
4 eggs
salt and pepper, to taste (optional)

1. Preheat the oven to 400°F.

2. Place the tomatoes in a roasting pan, sprinkle with the oil and salt and pepper, if using, and roast in the preheated oven for 20 minutes.

3. Meanwhile, add the sesame seeds, pumpkin seeds, and sunflower seeds to a skillet and dry-fry for 2–3 minutes, until starting to turn golden. Set aside.

4. Remove the tomatoes from the oven, and put into a blender or food processor with the roasted red peppers and blend to a sauce, adding enough broth to loosen it.

5. Pour the sauce into a saucepan, add the beans, bring to a simmer, and simmer for 12–15 minutes.

6. Halfway through cooking, stir in the raisins, half the slivered almonds, and half the cilantro.

7. Meanwhile, toast the bread on both sides. Bring a skillet of water to a simmer. Break the eggs into a cup, one at a time, add to the pan, and poach for 4–5 minutes. Remove the eggs from the pan and drain well.

8. Place the slices of toast on four warm plates and spoon the beans over them. Top each serving with a poached egg and sprinkle with the remaining almonds and cilantro, along with the toasted seeds.

Did you know that healthy snacking is a way of fitting extra nutrients into your diet, and that lunch keeps your metabolism active? We've taken this firmly to heart and so you'll feel the benefits once you've sampled this eclectic range of health-boosting recipes—from Maple Tofu with Egg-Fried Rice and Roasted Stuffed Pepper Poppers to a Protein Rice Bowl and Kale & Green Garlic Bruschetta.

ENERGY BOOST

Garlic & Herb Labneh

Serves: 4 | Prep: 20 minutes, plus 24 hours chilling | Cook: none

Per serving : 194 CAL | 12.8G FAT | 3.9G SAT FAT | 12G CARBS | 6.5G SUGAR | 2.6G FIBER | 9.4G PROTEIN | 40MG SODIUM

Labneh is a simple dip made by straining plain yogurt overnight to reduce its whey content. After that you can add your own flavors, using herbs and spices of your choice. Greek-style yogurt is a great source of protein and healthy probiotics, which are important for digestive health.

Ingredients

1¼ cups Greek-style yogurt

1 garlic clove, crushed

2 tablespoons finely chopped fresh herbs, such as cilantro, parsley, and mint

2 tablespoons extra virgin olive oil

2 tablespoons chopped pistachio nuts

14 ounces freshly cut vegetable sticks, including asparagus, red bell pepper, baby zucchini, baby corn, baby carrots, and baby broccoli

salt and pepper, to taste (optional)

1. The labneh needs to be made the day before serving. Line a strainer with a piece of cheesecloth and place the strainer over a bowl.

2. Pour in the yogurt and chill in the refrigerator for 24 hours. Squeeze the cheesecloth occasionally to help it along. The yogurt remaining in the cheesecloth will have a cheeselike consistency—this is the labneh.

3. Stir the garlic and herbs into the labneh and season with salt and pepper, if using.

4. Divide among four bowls, drizzle with oil, and sprinkle with chopped nuts. Serve with vegetable sticks for dipping.

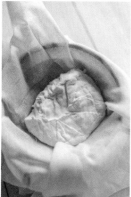

Root Veg Chips with Yogurt Dip

Serves: 4 | Prep: 30 minutes | Cook: 16 minutes, plus chilling

Per serving: 320 CAL | 16.4G FAT | 3.7G SAT FAT | 37.7G CARBS | 14.7G SUGAR | 8.4G FIBER | 7.8G PROTEIN | 720MG SODIUM

Making your own chips is surprisingly easy and you can be certain there are no added artificial flavorings or preservatives.

Ingredients

2¼ pounds mixed root vegetables, such as carrots, parsnips or sweet potatoes, and golden beets, thinly sliced

¼ cup virgin olive oil

sea salt and pepper, to taste (optional)

Herbed Garlic Dip

1 cup Greek-style plain yogurt

2 garlic cloves, finely chopped

¼ cup finely chopped fresh herbs, such as flat-leaf parsley, chives, basil, and oregano

1. Preheat the oven to 400°F. To make the herbed garlic dip, spoon the yogurt into a small bowl, then stir in the garlic and herbs and season with salt and pepper, if using. Cover and chill in the refrigerator.

2. Put the vegetables into a large bowl. Slowly drizzle the oil over them, gently turning the vegetables as you work, until they are all coated.

3. Arrange the vegetables over three baking sheets in a single layer, then season with salt and pepper, if using. Bake for 8–10 minutes, then check—the slices in the corners of the sheets will cook more quickly, so transfer any that are crisp and golden to a wire rack. Cook the rest for an additional 2–3 minutes, then transfer any additional cooked chips to the wire rack. Cook the remaining slices for another 2–3 minutes if needed, then transfer to the wire rack and let cool.

4. Arrange the chips in a bowl, spoon the dip into a smaller bowl, and serve.

Find Your Roots

Root vegetables grown in rich soil are full of nutrients and are an excellent source of fiber. Many, such as carrots and onions, are high in vitamin C, the B vitamins, and vitamin A. Others—for example, potatoes and beets—are rich in antioxidants.

Flavored Quinoa Balls

Serves: 24 | Prep: 35 minutes, plus chilling | Cook: 35 minutes

Per ball : 52 CAL | 3.1G FAT | 1.3G SAT FAT | 4.3G CARBS | 0.8G SUGAR | 1.9G FIBER | 2G PROTEIN | 120MG SODIUM

**One recipe and three magnificent flavors—these superpower balls
are a great get-ahead snack. You can cook a big batch to carry on the go.**

Ingredients

⅔ cup quinoa

1½ cups boiling water

3 tomatoes, halved

2 garlic cloves, finely chopped

2 teaspoons torn fresh thyme leaves

2 tablespoons virgin olive oil

4 cups young spinach leaves,
rinsed and drained

1¼ cups finely grated feta cheese

pinch of grated nutmeg

¼ cup finely chopped, pitted
black ripe olives

1 tablespoon chopped fresh basil

sea salt and pepper,
to taste (optional)

sweet chili relish,
to serve (optional)

1. Add the quinoa and water to a medium saucepan, cover, and cook over medium heat, stirring occasionally, for about 20 minutes, or according to package directions, until the quinoa is soft and has absorbed all the water.

2. Meanwhile, preheat the broiler. Arrange the tomatoes, cut side up, on the bottom of an aluminum foil-lined broiler rack. Sprinkle with the garlic, thyme, and a little salt and pepper, if using, then drizzle with 1 tablespoon of the oil and broil for 10 minutes.

3. Add the spinach to a dry, nonstick skillet and cook for 2–3 minutes, until just wilted. Scoop out of the pan and finely chop, then mix with one-third of the quinoa, one-third of the cheese, the nutmeg, and salt and pepper to taste, if using.

4. Peel the tomatoes, chop, and add with any pan juices to the empty spinach pan. Stir in half the remaining quinoa and cook for 2–3 minutes, until the mixture can be shaped into a ball. Remove from the heat and stir in half the remaining cheese.

5. Mix the remaining quinoa and cheese with the olives, basil, and a little salt and pepper, if using. Shape each of the flavored quinoa mixtures into eight small balls. Chill until ready to serve.

6. Preheat the oven to 350°F. Brush a roasting pan with the remaining oil, add the quinoa balls, and bake for 10 minutes, turning once, until the edges are golden brown and the cheese has melted. Serve hot or cold with sweet chili relish, if using, for dipping. Transfer the cooled quinoa balls to an airtight container, refrigerate, and eat within two to three days.

Why Not Try?

Instead of shrimp, you can use shredded pork or chicken. Always use fresh herbs—mint, cilantro, dill, and parsley all work well.

Vietnamese Summer Roll Bowl

Serves: 4 | Prep: 20 minutes | Cook: 4–5 minutes

Per serving: 426 CAL | 7.3G FAT | 1.4G SAT FAT | 59.2G CARBS | 9.8G SUGAR | 4.5G FIBER | 30.8G PROTEIN | 1,880MG SODIUM

Vietnamese summer rolls consist of crunchy, fresh raw vegetables, soft aromatic greens, succulent shrimp, and, in this case, light rice noodles. Deconstructed and served with a spicy piquant sauce, this is a perfect summer lunch dish.

Ingredients

7 ounces rice vermicelli noodles

1½ tablespoons sugar

¼ cup lime juice

2 tablespoons Thai fish sauce

2 garlic cloves, crushed

1 fresh Thai chile, finely sliced

20 mint leaves

20 cilantro leaves

8 fresh Thai basil sprigs, leaves only

8 snipped fresh chives

16 large cooked jumbo shrimp

1 carrot, shredded

½ cucumber, cut into thin matchsticks

2 Boston or other small butter lettuce, leaves separated

¼ cup chopped salted peanuts

1. Put the noodles into a large bowl and pour boiling water over them. Let soak for 4–5 minutes, or according to package directions, then rinse in cold water and drain.

2. Meanwhile, whisk together the sugar, lime juice, Thai fish sauce, garlic, and chile until the sugar is dissolved.

3. Toss the noodles with the herbs, then divide among four bowls.

4. Top with the remaining ingredients, then pour the sauce over them to serve.

Asian Spiced Edamame & Cranberries

Serves: 4 | Prep: 15 minutes, plus chilling | Cook: 15 minutes

Per serving : 183 CAL | 9.1G FAT | 1G SAT FAT | 12.8G CARBS | 7.4G SUGAR | 4.3G FIBER | 11.4G PROTEIN | 240MG SODIUM

This snack is packed with healthy goodness—edamame (soybeans) are low in fat and high in protein, fiber, and many other essential vitamins and minerals.

Ingredients

2¼ cups frozen edamame (green soybeans)

2-inch piece fresh ginger, peeled and finely grated

1 teaspoon Sichuan peppercorns, coarsely crushed

1 tablespoon soy sauce

1 tablespoon olive oil

3 small star anise or 1⅓ teaspoons five-spice powder

¼ cup dried cranberries

1. Preheat the oven to 350°F. Put the beans into a roasting pan, then sprinkle with the ginger and peppercorns. Drizzle with soy sauce and oil, and mix together.

2. Tuck the star anise in among the beans, or sprinkle with the five-spice powder, then roast, uncovered, in the preheated oven, for 15 minutes.

3. Stir in the cranberries and let cool. Spoon into a small jar and eat within 12 hours.

Bok Choy

The leafy vegetable bok choy is low in calories and packed full of other nutrients that benefit your health. These include phytonutrients, vitamins (particularly vitamins A and C), minerals, and a rich combination of antioxidants, which can help protect against breast, colon, and prostate cancers, and reduce LDL, or "bad cholesterol," levels in the blood.

Maple Tofu with Egg-Fried Rice

Serves: 4 | Prep: 10 minutes | Cook: 20 minutes

Per serving : 614 CAL | 29.4G FAT | 11.9G SAT FAT | 63.8G CARBS | 11.5G SUGAR | 6.87G FIBER | 27G PROTEIN | 760MG SODIUM

Tofu is a great source of vegetarian protein, and it is also a versatile ingredient—it can be marinated before cooking or cooked, as here, in a tasty maple sauce.

Ingredients

1 egg

2 teaspoons sesame oil

3 tablespoons coconut oil

1 cup long-grain rice, cooked

½ teaspoon ground turmeric

⅔ cup frozen peas, thawed

4 scallions, finely chopped

1 cup bean sprouts

⅓ cup cashew nuts

11¾ ounces tofu, drained and dried on paper towels

3 garlic cloves, crushed

3 tablespoons soy sauce

2 tablespoons maple syrup

1 tablespoon rice vinegar

3 bok choy, quartered lengthwise

2 tablespoons sesame seeds, toasted

1. Beat together the egg and sesame oil and set aside. Heat 2 tablespoons of the coconut oil in a wok or large skillet, add the rice and turmeric, and stir-fry for 3–4 minutes.

2. Add the peas, scallions, bean sprouts, and cashew nuts and stir–fry for 3 minutes.

3. Push the rice to one side of the wok, pour in the egg mixture, and let set for a few seconds, then move it around with chopsticks to break it up. Stir into the rice, then remove from the heat and cover while you cook the tofu.

4. Heat the remaining coconut oil in a skillet, add the tofu, and cook for 4–5 minutes, turning frequently, until lightly browned.

5. Mix together the garlic, soy sauce, maple syrup, and vinegar, add to the tofu, and cook, stirring occasionally, for 2–3 minutes, until the sauce thickens. Meanwhile, steam the bok choy.

6. Divide the rice among four warm bowls, top with the bok choy and maple tofu, sprinkle with the sesame seeds, and serve immediately.

Why Not Try?

If you prefer to eat meat, the tofu can be substituted with chunks of chicken—however, the cooking time may need to be a little longer.

Sweet Roots Bowl

Serves: 4 | Prep: 12 minutes | Cook: 35–40 minutes

Per serving : 402 CAL | 18.4G FAT | 2.3G SAT FAT | 54.2G CARBS | 11.8G SUGAR | 9.5G FIBER | 10.1G PROTEIN | 120MG SODIUM

Root vegetables are full of starch and sugar, so they're great for giving your energy levels a long-term boost. Using tahini in dressings increases your intake of protein and essential fats, both extremely important in a healthy diet.

Ingredients

2 sweet potatoes, cut into chunks

2 beets, cut into chunks

2 red onions, cut into wedges

2 tablespoons olive oil

2 teaspoons cumin seeds

⅓ cup brown rice

¼ cup tahini

juice of 1 lemon

⅛ teaspoon pepper

⅛ teaspoon honey

3 cups shredded kale

2 tablespoons slivered almonds, toasted

1. Preheat the oven to 400°F.

2. Put the sweet potatoes, beets, and onions into a bowl with the oil and cumin seeds and toss together to coat with the oil.

3. Transfer to a roasting pan and roast in the preheated oven for 35–40 minutes, until tender.

4. Meanwhile, cook the rice according to the package directions.

5. Whisk together the tahini, lemon juice, pepper, and honey.

6. Stir the kale into the root vegetables 10 minutes before the end of the roasting time.

7. Drain the rice and divide among four warm bowls.

8. Toss the vegetables with the dressing and serve on top of the rice, sprinkled with the almonds.

Kale & Green Garlic Bruschetta

Serves: 4 | Prep: 25 minutes | Cook: 25 minutes

Per serving : 278 CAL | 1.3G FAT | 1.7G SAT FAT | 35.4G CARBS | 3.6G SUGAR | 4.8G FIBER | 7.3G PROTEIN | 560MG SODIUM

Green, or "wet," garlic is the garlic from the first crop of the season. Soft and delicious, it is excellent spread on multigrain toast.

Ingredients

1 green garlic bulb

3 tablespoons olive oil

4 slices sourdough bread with mixed seeds

1¼ cups shredded kale

1 tablespoon balsamic vinegar

2 teaspoons pomegranate molasses

sea salt and pepper, to taste (optional)

1. Preheat the oven to 375°F. Put the garlic bulb on a piece of aluminum foil, drizzle with 1 tablespoon of the oil, then wrap the foil around it and seal well. Put on a baking sheet and roast in the preheated oven for 20 minutes, or until the bulb feels soft when squeezed.

2. Meanwhile, preheat a ridged grill pan. Cut the bread slices in half, brush one side of each with a little oil, then cook the bread, oiled side down, in the hot pan for 2 minutes. Brush the top with the remaining oil, then turn and cook the second side until golden brown.

3. Unwrap the garlic, peel away the outer casing from the bulb, separate the cloves, then remove any of the tougher skins. Crush the creamy soft garlic to a coarse paste, using a mortar and pestle. Mix the paste with any juices from the foil, then thinly spread on the grilled bread and keep warm.

4. Heat a dry, nonstick skillet, add the kale, and cook over medium heat for 2–3 minutes, until just wilted. Mix in the vinegar, molasses, and a little salt and pepper, if using. Arrange the bruschetta on a cutting board, spoon the kale on top, and serve.

Quinoa Salad in a Jar

Makes: 12 small jars or 6 large jars | Prep: 15 minutes | Cook: 15 minutes

Per serving : 534 CAL | 38.2G FAT | 7.3G SAT FAT | 38.1G CARBS | 5.3G SUGAR | 5.9G FIBER | 13.1G PROTEIN | 280MG SODIUM

Canning jars are the perfect way to show off the bright, fresh colors of this hearty salad, and it makes the recipe easy to take as a packed lunch.

Ingredients

1½ cups red or golden quinoa

4 scallions, thinly sliced

2 cups sliced, hulled fresh strawberries

¾ cup crumbled fresh goat cheese

⅔ cup roasted unsalted pistachio nuts, chopped

handful of fresh mint leaves, chopped

Dressing

⅓ cup lemon juice

1 teaspoon honey

1 teaspoon Dijon mustard

½ teaspoon salt

½ teaspoon pepper

⅔ cup olive oil

1. Cook the quinoa according to the package directions and let cool.

2. To make the dressing, put the lemon juice, honey, mustard, salt, and pepper into a small screw-top jar, secure the lid, and shake, or put the ingredients into a bowl and whisk to combine. Add the oil and shake or whisk vigorously until emulsified.

3. Toss 3 tablespoons of the dressing with the cooked quinoa.

4. To compose the salads, place 1 tablespoon of the dressing in each of twelve 8-ounce, wide-mouth canning jars, or place 2 tablespoons of the dressing in each of six 16-ounce wide-mouth canning jars. Add a layer of quinoa to each jar. Sprinkle with the scallions, add a layer of strawberries, a layer of cheese, and a layer of nuts, then top with mint. Spoon a little more dressing over the top and serve immediately.

Spicy Chicken Noodle Soup

Serves: 2 | Prep: 15 minutes | Cook: 5–10 minutes

Per serving : 511 CAL | 7.9G FAT | 2.3G SAT FAT | 66.4G CARBS | 7G SUGAR | 7.1G FIBER | 41.3G PROTEIN | 1,000MG SODIUM

This quick, healthy, wholesome soup is a real winner, creating an instant meal that's packed with goodness. The main flavor comes from miso, a highly nutritious fermented paste that is used as the basis of many noodle soups.

Ingredients

1¼ cups chicken broth

1 cup boiling water

1 (1¾-ounce) envelope miso paste

¾-inch piece fresh ginger, peeled and finely grated

1 red chile, seeded and thinly sliced

1 carrot, peeled and cut into thin strips

3 cups coarsely chopped bok choy

5½ ounces dried egg cellophane noodles, cooked

1 cooked chicken breast, shredded

dark soy sauce, to taste (optional)

4 scallions, trimmed and finely chopped

handful fresh cilantro, coarsely chopped, to serve

1. Put the broth and boiling water in a saucepan and bring to a boil over medium–high heat. Add the miso paste and simmer for 1–2 minutes.

2. Add the ginger, chile, carrot, bok choy, cooked noodles, and chicken. Simmer for an additional 4–5 minutes. Season with soy sauce, if using.

3. Sprinkle the scallions in the bottom of two warm serving bowls and pour the soup over them. Top with chopped cilantro and serve immediately.

Mexican Beef & Bean Bowl

Serves: 4 | Prep: 10 minutes | Cook: 20–25 minutes

Per serving: 682 CAL | 25.4G FAT | 8.7G SAT FAT | 69.6G CARBS | 8.7G SUGAR | 11.3G FIBER | 37.9G PROTEIN | 200MG SODIUM

Chili con carne with extra beans for protein and fiber, plus red bell peppers for their great flavor and antioxidant content, make a perfect dish—prepare in advance, because the flavors improve over time.

Ingredients

1 tablespoon olive oil

1 pound 2 ounces ground round beef

1 onion, chopped

2 red bell peppers, seeded and sliced

2⅓ teaspoons chili powder

1½ cups rinsed and drained, canned red kidney beans

1½ cups rinsed and drained canned cannellini beans

1⅔ cups canned diced tomatoes

1 tablespoon tomato paste

½ cup vegetable broth

1 cup basmati or other long-grain rice

2 tablespoons chopped fresh cilantro

2 tablespoons sour cream

¼ teaspoon smoked paprika

salt and pepper, to taste (optional)

1. Heat the oil in a large skillet, add the ground beef, and cook for 2–3 minutes, until brown all over.

2. Add the onion and red bell peppers and cook, stirring occasionally, for 3–4 minutes.

3. Stir in the chili powder and cook for 1 minute, then add the kidney beans, cannellini white kidney beans, tomatoes, tomato paste, and broth. Bring to a simmer and simmer for 12–15 minutes. Season with salt and pepper, if using.

4. Meanwhile, cook the rice according to the package directions.

5. Stir the cilantro into the chili and serve in warm bowls with the rice, topped with a dollop of sour cream and a sprinkling of the paprika.

Why Not Try?

If you are vegetarian, you can omit the ground meat altogether and make your chili with beans and tomato sauce, adding plenty of spice and chopped herbs for extra flavor.

Sweet Potato

The orange-fleshed sweet potato is high in carotenes and cholesterol-lowering compounds and is an ideal food for dieters. Sweet potatoes are richer in nutrients than potatoes and lower on the glycemic index. High in beta-carotene, they are an excellent source of vitamin E, magnesium, potassium, and selenium. Steaming them is a good way to maximize their nutritional value.

Greek Salad Crostini

Serves: 2 | Prep: 10 minutes | Cook: 5 minutes

Per serving : 379 CAL | 28.8G FAT | 9.7G SAT FAT | 20.2G CARBS | 6.7G SUGAR | 3.6G FIBER | 11.5G PROTEIN | 1,120MG SODIUM

Crisp toasted country-style bread topped with a salad that packs in the flavors is a really easy option for a quick-and-tasty lunch.

Ingredients

1 garlic clove, crushed

¼ cup olive oil

2 thick slices from a large, seeded loaf of bread

1⅓ cups diced vegetarian feta cheese

¼ cucumber, finely diced

¼ cup sliced black ripe olives

4 plum tomatoes, diced

½ small onion, chopped

2 fresh mint sprigs, shredded

2 fresh oregano sprigs, chopped

¼ teaspoon sugar

1 Boston or other small butter lettuce heart, finely shredded

⅓ teaspoon toasted sesame seeds

2 teaspoons pine nuts (optional)

pepper, to taste (optional)

1. Preheat the broiler to medium–high. Mix the garlic and oil in a bowl large enough to mix together all the salad ingredients.

2. To make the crostini, place the bread on the rack in the broiler pan. Lightly brush with the garlic oil and toast well away from the heat for 2–3 minutes, until crisp and golden. Turn the bread and lightly brush with more oil, then toast again.

3. Add the feta cheese to the garlic oil remaining in the bowl and season with pepper, if using (the cheese and olives usually provide enough salt). Mix in the cucumber, olives, tomatoes, onion, mint, and oregano. Sprinkle with the sugar and mix well. Finally, lightly mix in the lettuce.

4. Transfer the crostini to plates and spoon the salad and its juices over them. Sprinkle with the sesame seeds and pine nuts, if using, and serve immediately, while the crostini are hot and crisp.

Rainbow Power Rolls

Serves: 4 | Prep: 15 minutes | Cook: none

Per serving: 218 CAL | 2.6G FAT | 0.4G SAT FAT | 39.3G CARBS | 6G SUGAR | 6G FIBER | 8.7G PROTEIN | 280MG SODIUM

These rolls, full of color and great nutrient-rich ingredients, make a perfect packed lunch for work or for a picnic. Alfalfa sprouts are a great source of fiber and protein, but if you can't get them, any sprouts will do—they are all healthy.

Ingredients

4 multigrain rolls
¼ cup hummus
1 large carrot, grated
6 radishes, thinly sliced
½ red bell pepper, seeded and sliced
½ yellow bell pepper, seeded and sliced
2 tablespoons frozen corn kernels, thawed
2 tablespoons frozen peas, thawed
2 tablespoons alfalfa sprouts

1. Slice each roll across the middle horizontally, and spread the bottom half with hummus.

2. Divide the remaining ingredients among the rolls and replace the tops to serve.

Why Not Try?

If you can't get salmon, try using a white fish such as cod or halibut—both work well in this recipe.

Salmon
Burrito Bowl

Serves: 4 | Prep: 20 minutes | Cook: 20 minutes

Per serving: 716 CAL | 26.2G FAT | 8.4G SAT FAT | 78G CARBS | 23.7G SUGAR | 7.7G FIBER | 40.3G PROTEIN | 760MG SODIUM

Salmon is a great source of essential fats, as well as being rich in protein. Served here with rice and beans, which are also rich in protein, this recipe provides a real protein boost to your day. Dietary guidelines recommend eating oily fish at least two or three times a week, so this is a great way to get your essential fats.

Ingredients

1 tablespoon coconut oil

2 garlic cloves, crushed

1 red onion, peeled and diced

1 celery stalk, diced

1 red bell pepper, seeded and diced

1½ cups rinsed and drained, canned red kidney beans

1 cup long-grain rice

2⅓ cups vegetable broth

2 tablespoons jerk paste

2 tablespoons honey

4 salmon fillets, about 5½ ounces each

Mango Salsa

1 large mango, peeled, pitted, and diced

½ red onion, finely diced

2 tablespoons chopped fresh cilantro

juice of 1 lime

1. To make the mango salsa, mix together the mango, onion, cilantro, and lime juice and let stand at room temperature.

2. Meanwhile, heat the coconut oil in a large saucepan, add the garlic, onion, celery, and red bell pepper, and sauté for 4–5 minutes. Add the kidney beans to the pan.

3. Add the rice and broth, bring to a boil, cover, and simmer for about 15 minutes, until the rice is tender and the liquid has been absorbed.

4. Meanwhile, mix together the jerk paste and honey. Preheat the broiler to hot and line a baking sheet with aluminum foil. Place the salmon fillets on the prepared sheet and spread the jerk mixture over each one.

5. Cook the salmon fillets under the broiler for 8–10 minutes, turning once.

6. Serve the rice in warm bowls, topped with a fillet of salmon and some mango salsa.

Protein Rice Bowl

Serves: 2 | Prep: 25 minutes | Cook: 30 minutes

Per serving : 653 CAL | 33.9G FAT | 5.9G SAT FAT | 71.1G CARBS | 4G SUGAR | 8.7G FIBER | 19.1G PROTEIN | 120MG SODIUM

Brown rice adds important fiber and fresh chile supplies a kick of heat to this protein-rich vegetarian lunch for two.

Ingredients

¾ cup brown rice

2 extra-large eggs

2½ cups spinach

4 scallions, finely chopped

1 red chile, seeded and finely sliced

½ ripe avocado, sliced

2 tablespoons roasted peanuts

Vinaigrette

2 tablespoons olive oil

1 teaspoon Dijon mustard

1 tablespoon apple cider vinegar

juice of ½ a lemon

1. Put the rice into a large saucepan and cover with twice the volume of water. Bring to a boil and simmer for 25 minutes, or according to package directions, until the rice is tender and the liquid has nearly all disappeared. Continue to simmer for an additional few minutes if some liquid remains.

2. Meanwhile, cook your eggs. Bring a small saucepan of water to a boil. Carefully add the eggs to the pan and boil for 7 minutes—the whites will be cooked and the yolks should still be slightly soft. Drain and pour cold water over the eggs to stop them from cooking. When cool enough to handle, tap them on the work surface to crack the shells and peel them. Cut the eggs into quarters.

3. Stir the spinach, half of the scallions, and some of the red chile into the cooked rice.

4. To make the vinaigrette, whisk together the olive oil, Dijon mustard, apple cider vinegar, and lemon juice. Pour the dressing over the warm rice and mix to combine.

5. Divide the rice between two bowls and top each with the remaining scallions, avocado, remaining red chile, peanuts, and egg quarters.

Turkey & Rainbow Chard Roll-Ups

Makes: 8 | Prep: 30–35 minutes, plus chilling | Cook: none

Per serving: 104 CAL | 6.1G FAT | 1G SAT FAT | 17.5G CARBS | 1.6G SUGAR | 3.6G FIBER | 6.5G PROTEIN | 200MG SODIUM

Turkey is a rich source of protein. It's also a versatile ingredient, because it complements fruits, vegetables, and bread products. Here, we've added plenty of nutrient-rich vegetables to the mix.

Ingredients

8 rainbow Swiss chard leaves and stems (choose leaves that are about the same size as the slices of turkey), the stems cut into matchstick strips

8 thin slices cooked turkey

⅔ cup hummus

2 scallions, trimmed and cut into fine strips

1 carrot, cut into matchstick strips

½ zucchini, cut into matchstick strips

1 avocado, halved, pitted, peeled, and thinly sliced

juice of 1 lemon

1. Separate the Swiss chard leaves and arrange, shiny side down, on a large cutting board. Cover each one with a slice of turkey, then spread the turkey with a little hummus.

2. Divide the Swiss chard stems, scallions, carrot, and zucchini among the chard leaves, making a little pile on each leaf that runs in the center of the leaf from long edge to long edge.

3. Top the little mounds with the avocado slices and a little lemon juice, then roll up from the bottom of the leaf to the tip and put on a plate, with the seam facing down. Continue until all the leaves have been rolled.

4. Cut each roll into thick slices and transfer to individual plates, or wrap each roll in plastic wrap and chill for up to 1 hour.

Why Not Try?

For a higher-carb, preworkout version
of this dish, replace the Swiss chard
with whole wheat tortillas.

Roasted Stuffed Pepper Poppers

Makes: 12 | Prep: 30–35 minutes | Cook: 15 minutes

Per stuffed pepper : 59 CAL | 3.2G FAT | 1.5G SAT FAT | 2.4G CARBS | 1.7G SUGAR | 0.7G FIBER | 5G PROTEIN | 160MG SODIUM

Filled with oozing cheese, these tasty little mouthfuls are perfect for serving as appetizers for a dinner party.

Ingredients

olive oil, for oiling

⅓ cup cream cheese

2 garlic cloves, finely chopped

2 teaspoons finely chopped fresh rosemary

1 tablespoon finely chopped fresh basil

1 tablespoon finely chopped fresh parsley

3 tablespoons finely grated fresh Parmesan cheese

1 cup finely chopped cooked chicken breast

3 scallions, finely chopped

12 mixed colored baby bell peppers

sea salt and pepper, to taste (optional)

1. Preheat the oven to 375°F. Lightly brush a large baking sheet with oil.

2. Put the cream cheese, garlic, rosemary, basil, and parsley into a bowl, then add the Parmesan and stir together with a metal spoon.

3. Mix in the chicken and scallions, then season with a little salt and pepper, if using.

4. Slit each bell pepper from the tip up to the stem, leaving the stem in place, then make a small cut just to the side, so that you can get a teaspoon into the center of the bell pepper to scoop out the seeds.

5. Fill each bell pepper with some of the chicken mixture, then place on the prepared baking sheet. Cook in the preheated oven for 15 minutes, or until the bell peppers are soft and light brown in patches.

6. Let cool slightly on the baking sheet, then transfer to a serving plate. Serve warm or cold. These are best eaten on the day they are made and should be kept in the refrigerator if serving cold.

Eating meat and fish is an easy way of keeping up with our recommended two to three portions of protein a day. But do abandon any forced thoughts of "I-must-eat-fish-or-meat-because-it's-good-for-me" and take a walk on the wild side. Ranging from a Broccoli, Cauliflower & Beef Stir-Fry to Gingered Steak Lettuce Boats, and a Sushi Roll Bowl to a Pesto Salmon with Spring Veg Bowl, it's time to be hungry.

PROTEIN PACKED

Chicken & Garbanzo Bean Power Bowl

Serves: 4 | Prep: 45 minutes | Cook: 35–40 minutes

Per serving : 450 CAL | 20.8G FAT | 3.9G SAT FAT | 35G CARBS | 13G SUGAR | 8.1G FIBER | 30.6G PROTEIN | 160MG SODIUM

Chicken and garbanzo beans are both rich in protein, so this recipe will give you a double boost. With a great peanut dressing, this one is hard to resist.

Ingredients

1½ cups rinsed and drained, canned garbanzo beans

½ butternut squash, peeled, seeded, and chopped into bite-size pieces

2 red bell peppers, seeded and chopped

1 red onion, coarsely chopped

3 tablespoons olive oil

½ teaspoon paprika

½ teaspoon cumin seeds

2 large chicken breasts

½ teaspoon peanut oil

1 garlic clove, crushed

½ teaspoon crushed red pepper flakes

1½ teaspoons packed light brown sugar

1 teaspoon soy sauce

2 tablespoons smooth peanut butter

1¼ cups coconut milk

20 sprigs of watercress or 1¾ cups other peppery greens, to serve

1. Preheat the oven to 400°F.

2. Put the garbanzo beans, squash, red bell peppers, and onion into two roasting pans, add 1 tablespoon of the olive oil to each pan, and toss to coat the vegetables. Roast in the preheated oven for 30–35 minutes, until the vegetables are tender and charred at the edges.

3. Meanwhile, mix the remaining olive oil with the paprika and cumin seeds.

4. Place the chicken between two sheets of wax paper and flatten slightly with a rolling pin or mallet (this helps them to cook more evenly).

5. Rub the chicken with the spiced oil. Preheat a ridged grill pan to hot.

6. Add the chicken to the hot pan and cook for 4–5 minutes on each side, until cooked through. Let rest for 1–2 minutes, then cut into strips.

7. Meanwhile, heat the peanut oil in a saucepan, add the garlic and crushed red pepper flakes, and cook for 30 seconds, then add the sugar and cook for 1 minute. Stir in the soy sauce and peanut butter, then add the coconut milk, a little at a time, stirring constantly, until the sauce has the consistency you prefer.

8. Serve the roasted vegetables and garbanzo beans on a bed of watercress in four bowls, topped with strips of chicken and the sauce.

Lamb & Pumpkin with Udon Noodles

Serves: 4 | Prep: 10 minutes | Cook: 30 minutes

Per serving : 942 CAL | 53.9G FAT | 30.9G SAT FAT | 85.7G CARBS | 15.9G SUGAR | 3.2G FIBER | 31.3G PROTEIN | 2,360MG SODIUM

Udon noodles are perfect for soaking up this rich, spicy sauce. Full-flavored lamb makes this dish especially satisfying, but you can also substitute beef, pork, or chicken.

Ingredients

2 tablespoons vegetable oil

2 shallots, thinly sliced

1 pound boneless lamb shoulder, cut into 1-inch cubes

1–2 tablespoons Thai red curry paste

1 (14-ounce) can coconut milk

1 cup vegetable, beef, or chicken broth or water

3 tablespoons Thai fish sauce

2 tablespoons packed light brown sugar

3 lemongrass stalks, cut into 3-inch pieces and bruised with the side of a heavy knife

3 kaffir lime leaves, julienned

2 cups peeled and seeded, bite-size pumpkin or butternut squash cubes

12 ounces dried udon noodles

juice of 1 lime

¼ cup chopped fresh cilantro, to garnish

1. Heat the oil in a large, deep skillet over medium–high heat. Add the shallots and cook, stirring frequently, for 5 minutes, or until soft. Add the lamb and cook, stirring frequently, until brown all over. Stir in the curry paste and about 2 tablespoons of the thick cream at the top of the can of coconut milk. Cook for 1 minute. Add the remaining coconut milk, the broth, fish sauce, sugar, lemongrass, and lime leaves. Bring to a boil and add the pumpkin. Reduce the heat to medium–low, cover, and simmer for 15–20 minutes, until the pumpkin is tender.

2. Meanwhile, cook the noodles according to the package directions. Drain and set aside.

3. When the pumpkin is tender, add the drained noodles to the pan and cook for 2–3 minutes, until heated through. Stir in the lime juice and serve immediately, garnished with the cilantro.

Broccoli, Cauliflower & Beef Stir-Fry

Serves: 4 | Prep: 8 minutes | Cook: 8–12 minutes

Per serving: 321 CAL | 16.9G FAT | 5.6G SAT FAT | 14.7G CARBS | 6.4G SUGAR | 4.2G FIBER | 29.3G PROTEIN | 520MG SODIUM

Stir-fries are great for making quick, healthy meals. Cooking at high temperatures tends to reduce nutrients, so instead aim to "steam-fry" by adding a little liquid and covering the wok or skillet for a few minutes to cook more gently.

Ingredients

zest and juice of 1 orange

2 tablespoons soy sauce

2 tablespoons sesame oil

2¾ cups trimmed baby broccoli

1½ cups cauliflower florets

1 tablespoon coconut oil

2-inch piece fresh ginger, peeled and shredded

1 garlic clove, peeled and sliced

1 red chile, seeded and diced

14 ounces tenderloin steak, cut into thin strips

1 red bell pepper, seeded and thinly sliced

½ cup shredded snow peas

2 tablespoons sesame seeds, toasted

1. Mix together the orange zest and juice, soy sauce, and sesame oil in a bowl.

2. Bring a large saucepan of water to a boil, add the broccoli and cauliflower, and blanch for 2 minutes, then drain.

3. Heat the coconut oil in a wok or large skillet and add the ginger, garlic, chile, and steak and stir-fry until the steak is brown all over. Remove with a slotted spoon.

4. Add the red bell pepper, snow peas, baby broccoli, and cauliflower, pour in the orange juice mixture, cover, and cook for 2–3 minutes.

5. Return the steak to the wok and stir-fry for 1–2 minutes, then serve in warm bowls, sprinkled with the toasted sesame seeds.

Meat the Best

Always choose a good-quality cut of meat, especially when cooking the meat quickly, as in this recipe. It is also great served with egg noodles, if you need more carbs.

Turkey

A low-fat protein source, turkey helps promote a positive outlook as well as high levels of energy and vitality. It is known for its high tryptophan content, a protein constituent from which the body makes the mood, sleep, and appetite-regulating brain chemical serotonin. Turkey's high-protein content also helps control appetite by balancing blood sugar levels, curbing sugar cravings and energy fluctuations.

Moroccan Lamb Burgers

Serves: 4 | Prep: 25–30 minutes, plus standing | Cook: 10–12 minutes

Per serving: 615 CAL | 36.5G FAT | 14.9G SAT FAT | 39.2G CARBS | 5.8G SUGAR | 3.8G FIBER | 30.2G PROTEIN | 200MG SODIUM

These tasty burgers with an easy-to-make yogurt relish are perfect for a healthy treat. Pita bread is used here, but they are also good with whole wheat bread.

Ingredients

1¼ pounds fresh ground lamb

1 onion, grated

1 teaspoon harissa sauce

1 garlic clove, crushed

2 tablespoons finely chopped fresh mint

½ teaspoon cumin seeds, crushed

½ teaspoon paprika

oil, for greasing

salt and pepper, to taste (optional)

Yogurt Sauce

½ large cucumber

¼ cup plain yogurt

⅓ cup chopped fresh mint

salt (optional)

To Serve

4 pita breads, warmed

½ red onion, halved and thinly sliced

1⅓ cups shredded lettuce

1. To make the sauce, peel the cucumber, quarter it lengthwise, and scoop out the seeds. Chop the flesh and put into a strainer set over a bowl. Sprinkle with salt, if using, cover with a plate, and weigh down with a can of vegetables. Let drain for 30 minutes, then mix with the remaining ingredients.

2. Combine the lamb, onion, harissa sauce, garlic, mint, cumin seeds, and paprika. Season with salt and pepper, if using, mixing well with a fork. Divide into 4 balls and flatten into patties about 1 inch thick. Cover and let stand at room temperature for 30 minutes.

3. Preheat the barbecue grill. Lightly brush the patties with oil. Grease the grill rack. Cook over hot coals for 5–6 minutes on each side, or until cooked through.

4. Stuff the burgers into warm pita breads with the red onion, lettuce, and a spoonful of the sauce. Serve immediately.

Turkey Waldorf Bowl

Serves: 4 | Prep: 20 minutes | Cook: none

| Per serving: | 482CAL | 29.3G FAT | 3.4G SAT FAT | 29.1G CARBS | 17.4G SUGAR | 6.8G FIBER | 32.8G PROTEIN | 200MG SODIUM |

Turkey is a lean meat that is also high in protein, so it's great for a healthy, balanced diet. It is also rich in tryptophan, a precursor to the hormone serotonin, known as the "happy hormone." Paired with plenty of crunchy raw fruit and vegetables and tahini-and-lime dressing, this salad is hard to beat.

Ingredients

3 tablespoons tahini

2 tablespoons lime juice

2 teaspoons agave syrup

1 teaspoon soy sauce

2½ cups shredded, cooked turkey

2 celery stalks, thinly sliced

½ cup shredded red cabbage

2 crisp apples, cored and chopped

⅔ cup seedless red grapes, halved

1 cup shredded napa cabbage

⅓ cup walnuts, toasted

⅓ cup pecans, toasted

salt and pepper, to taste (optional)

1. Whisk together the tahini, lime juice, agave syrup, and soy sauce and season with salt and pepper, if using.

2. Lightly toss together the remaining ingredients, then toss again with the dressing. Divide among four large shallow bowls and serve immediately.

Why Not Try?

You can use chicken or even smoked mackerel in place of turkey in this salad. If you are using mackerel, try adding a little creamed horseradish to the dressing for a real kick.

Jerk Chicken with Papaya Salsa

Serves: 4 | Prep: 15 minutes | Cook: 35 minutes

Per serving : 394 CAL | 18.1G FAT | 3.2G SAT FAT | 17.1G CARBS | 5.4G SUGAR | 7.8G FIBER | 42G PROTEIN | 360MG SODIUM

Jamaica's jerk chicken is traditionally prepared by cooking the meat over fires made from the wood of the island's allspice trees. This one uses a Jamaican dry spice rub, which is not high in calories, and it can be done in your own kitchen.

Ingredients

2¾ pounds small chicken drumsticks, skinned

1 tablespoon olive oil

1 romaine lettuce, leaves separated and torn into pieces (optional)

3 cups baby spinach (optional)

Jerk Spice Rub

1 teaspoon allspice berries, crushed

1 teaspoon coriander seeds, crushed

1 teaspoon mild paprika

¼ teaspoon freshly grated nutmeg

1 tablespoon fresh thyme leaves

1 tablespoon black peppercorns, coarsely crushed

a pinch of salt

Salsa

1 papaya, halved, seeded, peeled, and cut into cubes

2 large avocados, pitted, peeled, and cut into cubes

finely grated zest and juice of 1 lime

½ red chile, seeded and finely chopped

½ red onion, finely chopped

⅓ cup finely chopped fresh cilantro

2 teaspoons chia seeds

1. Preheat the oven to 400°F. To make the jerk spice rub, mix together all the ingredients in a small bowl.

2. Slash each chicken drumstick two or three times with a knife, then put them into a roasting pan and drizzle with the oil. Sprinkle the spice mix over the chicken, then rub it in with your fingers, washing your hands well afterward. Roast the chicken for 30–35 minutes, or until browned with piping hot juices that run clear with no sign of pink when the tip of a sharp knife is inserted into the thickest part of a drumstick.

3. Meanwhile, to make the salsa, put the papaya and avocados into a bowl, sprinkle with the lime zest and juice, then toss well. Add the chile, red onion, cilantro, and chia seeds and stir.

4. Toss the lettuce and spinach together, if using. Serve with the chicken and salsa.

Gingered Steak Lettuce Boats

Serves: 4 | Prep: 15 minutes, plus 20 minutes marinating | Cook: 5 minutes

Per serving: 245 CAL | 8.6G FAT | 2.2G SAT FAT | 18G CARBS | 11.5G SUGAR | 3G FIBER | 26.1G PROTEIN | 520MG SODIUM

This recipe is a great way of serving food—the lettuce wraps, encasing all the wonderful flavors within, can be picked up with your fingers.

Ingredients

2 tablespoons soy sauce

2 tablespoons honey

1 teaspoon smooth mustard

2 garlic cloves, crushed

¼ cup peeled and finely diced fresh ginger

14 ounces sirloin steak, cut into strips

8 scallions, shredded

1 carrot, grated

¼ cucumber, cut into julienne strips

8 snow pea pods, cut into julienne strips

4 Boston or other small butter lettuce, leaves separated

small handful of fresh cilantro sprigs (optional)

2 tablespoons sesame seeds, toasted (optional)

1. Mix together the soy sauce, honey, mustard, garlic, and ginger in a small bowl.

2. Put the strips of steak into a nonmetallic bowl and pour the soy-and-honey mixture over them. Let marinate for at least 20 minutes.

3. Meanwhile, toss together the scallions, carrot, cucumber, and snow peas.

4. Preheat a ridged grill pan to hot, add the steak strips, and cook for 1–2 minutes, pouring the remaining marinade into the pan at the end of cooking to heat through.

5. Divide the steak among the lettuce leaves, then top with the salad ingredients, finishing with a sprig of cilantro and sprinkling of sesame seeds, if using. Drizzle with a little cooked marinade, if desired.

Rib-Eye Steak with Chimichurri

Serves: 2 | Prep: 30 minutes | Cook: 22 minutes

Per serving: 691 CAL | 52.8G FAT | 15.7G SAT FAT | 26.4G CARBS | 5.2G SUGAR | 3.8G FIBER | 27G PROTEIN | 800MG SODIUM

Chimichurri is an Argentinian herb sauce with a texture similar to coarse pesto. Most regions have a variation, such as adding anchovies or removing the chile.

Ingredients

1 tablespoon olive oil

2 rib-eye steaks, about 4½ ounces each

½ teaspoon ground cumin

sea salt and pepper, to taste (optional)

Chimichurri Sauce

⅓ cup coarsely chopped fresh flat-leaf parsley

2⅓ tablespoons fresh oregano

3 small garlic cloves, coarsely chopped

½ shallot, coarsely chopped

¼ red chile, seeded and coarsely chopped

3 tablespoons extra virgin olive oil

1 teaspoon red wine vinegar

juice of ¼ lemon

Sweet Potatoes

2 small sweet potatoes, cut into ¾-inch chunks

1½ tablespoons butter

1. For the sweet potatoes, put them into a large saucepan of lightly salted (if using salt) boiling water for 12–15 minutes, or until soft. Drain, then remove from the heat and steam-dry in the pan for at least 5 minutes. Using a potato masher, mash the potatoes to a smooth consistency.

2. Meanwhile, to make the chimichurri sauce, put all the ingredients into a food processor, season with salt and pepper, if using, and process until you have a paste of a similar consistency to pesto. Add a little extra olive oil if the mixture appears too thick. Spoon into a serving bowl, cover, and set aside.

3. Return the sweet potatoes to the heat and warm through before stirring in the butter. Season with salt and pepper, if using, and keep warm.

4. Massage the oil into both sides of each steak, and sprinkle with salt and the cumin. Heat a ridged grill pan over high heat until hot. Cook each steak for 2–3 minutes on each side, or for longer if you prefer it well done. Let the steaks rest for 2 minutes.

5. Serve a steak on each of two warm plates with the chimichurri sauce spooned over and the mashed sweet potatoes on the side.

Pan-Cooked Tuna with Radish Relish

Serves: 4 | Prep: 15 minutes, plus marinating | Cook: 10 minutes

Per serving : 279 CAL | 12.1G FAT | 1.5G SAT FAT | 2.2G CARBS | 1G SUGAR | 0.7G FIBER | 38.3G PROTEIN | 520MG SODIUM

Borrowing from the Japanese tradition of pickling vegetables, the radishes and cucumber are marinated in a delicious mix of sweet and sour, which goes particularly well with the tuna.

Ingredients

4 tuna steaks, about 5½ ounces each
1 tablespoon sesame seeds
cooked rice, to serve (optional)

Marinade

2 tablespoons dark soy sauce
2 tablespoons sunflower oil
1 tablespoon sesame oil
1 tablespoon rice vinegar
1 teaspoon grated fresh ginger

Relish

½ cucumber, peeled
1 bunch of red radishes, trimmed

1. Put the tuna steaks into a dish and sprinkle with the sesame seeds, pressing them in with the back of a spoon so they stick to the fish.

2. To make the marinade, whisk together all the ingredients. Transfer 3 tablespoons of the marinade to a medium bowl. Pour the remaining marinade over the fish, turning each steak to coat lightly. Cover and chill for 1 hour.

3. Slice the cucumber and radishes thinly and add to the marinade in the bowl. Toss the vegetables to coat, then cover and chill.

4. Heat a large, heavy skillet over high heat. Add the steaks and cook for 3–4 minutes on each side, depending on the thickness of the fish. Serve immediately with the radish relish and rice, if using.

Tune into Tuna

The health benefits of tuna fish include its ability to stimulate growth, lower blood pressure and cholesterol levels, boost the immune system, increase energy, increase our red blood cell count, and reduce general inflammation.

Tuna & Salmon

Fresh tuna is an important source of omega-3 fats and antioxidant minerals for arterial and heart health, and it is also rich in vitamin E for healthy skin. Salmon is an excellent source of omega-3 fats, cancer-fighting selenium, and vitamin B12, which helps protect against heart disease and chronic diseases, such as Alzheimer's disease, depression, and diabetes.

Sushi Roll Bowl

Serves: 4 | Prep: 15 minutes, plus cooling | Cook: 10 minutes

Per serving: 572 CAL | 17.7G FAT | 3.1G SAT FAT | 70.1G CARBS | 2.2G SUGAR | 7.6G FIBER | 32G PROTEIN | 960MG SODIUM

Sushi makes a great healthy snack or meal: the omega-3 fats in the fish are linked to heart protection and improved circulation; rice provides energy and protein; wasabi has been found to aid cancer prevention and prevent blood clots; and seaweed is rich in iodine—vital for a healthy thyroid. And it tastes great, too.

Ingredients

1⅔ cups glutinous rice

2 tablespoons rice vinegar

1 teaspoon sugar

1 large avocado, peeled, pitted, and sliced

7 ounces raw tuna, sliced

7 ounces raw salmon, sliced

juice of ½ lemon

4 sheets nori seaweed, shredded

¼ cucumber, cut into matchsticks

2 tablespoons snipped fresh chives

1 tablespoon black sesame seeds

¼ cup soy sauce, to serve

1. Cook the rice according to the package directions. When all the water has been absorbed and the rice is cooked, stir through the vinegar and sugar, then cover and let cool.

2. Divide the rice among four bowls.

3. Top each bowl with slices of avocado, tuna, and salmon.

4. Squeeze with the lemon juice, then add the nori, cucumber, chives, and sesame seeds.

5. Serve with the soy sauce.

Roasted Salmon with Pomegranate

Serves: 4 | Prep: 10 minutes | Cook: 15–20 minutes

Per serving : 316CAL | 19.4G FAT | 4.2G SAT FAT | 8.3G CARBS | 5.1G SUGAR | 2.2G FIBER | 26.3G PROTEIN | 720MG SODIUM

This spiced salmon makes a quick-and-easy midweek dinner, but it tastes spectacular enough for guests, too. Cooking salmon with pomegranate en papillote (in a package) gives the fish a wonderful sharpness and sweetness.

Ingredients

4 salmon fillets
2 teaspoons ras el hanout
1 teaspoon sea salt flakes
grated zest and juice of 1 lemon
2 teaspoons olive oil
⅓ pomegranate, seeds only
¼ cup coarsely chopped fresh cilantro

1. Preheat the oven to 350°F. Cut out four rectangles of parchment paper, each large enough to comfortably wrap a salmon fillet, and four slightly larger rectangles of aluminum foil. Lay each rectangle of parchment paper over a rectangle of foil. Put a salmon fillet in the center of each parchment paper rectangle.

2. Sprinkle the fillets with the ras el hanout, salt, lemon zest and juice, and oil, then the pomegranate seeds and cilantro. Bring the long edges of the parchment paper up together, before folding them down a few times to form a crisp pleat over the top of the salmon and tucking the short edges below. Repeat with the foil underneath to form a secure package.

3. Put the packages on a baking sheet. Roast on a high shelf for 15–20 minutes, or until the fish is cooked through and flakes easily when pressed with a knife. Serve the packages for people to unwrap at the table.

Salmon Suits

Salmon flesh is most often pink, but the color spectrum varies from red to orange. The fat and omega-3 content varies from one species to another, but all salmon provides a good source of high-quality protein and omega-3 fatty acids.

Pesto Salmon with Spring Veg Bowl

Serves: 4 | Prep: 15 minutes | Cook: 10–12 minutes

Per serving : 646 CAL | 42.9G FAT | 7.6G SAT FAT | 21.9G CARBS | 7.7G SUGAR | 9.7G FIBER | 42G PROTEIN | 280MG SODIUM

Spring vegetables are so tasty they really don't need much doing to them, just gentle steaming and a little lemon dressing. The lemon dressing cuts through the richness of the pesto salmon perfectly. Steaming food is perfect for retaining nutrients, because the cooking temperature is lower than when frying or boiling.

Ingredients

1⅓ cups fresh or frozen peas

1⅓ cups fresh fava beans

7 ounces asparagus, woody stems discarded

7 ounces baby carrots, scrubbed

4 skinless salmon fillets, about 5½ ounces each

¼ cup pesto

3 tablespoons extra virgin olive oil

grated zest and juice of 1 lemon

2 tablespoons sunflower seeds, toasted

2 tablespoons pumpkin seeds, toasted

2 tablespoons shredded fresh basil

1. Put all the vegetables into a steamer and cook for 10–12 minutes, until tender.

2. Meanwhile, preheat the broiler to hot and line a baking sheet with aluminum foil. Put the salmon onto the prepared baking sheet and spoon over the pesto. Cook under the broiler for 3–4 minutes on each side.

3. Mix the oil with the lemon zest and juice and toss with the cooked vegetables.

4. Divide the vegetables among four warm shallow bowls and top each one with a salmon fillet.

5. Sprinkle with the sunflower seeds, pumpkin seeds, and shredded basil and serve.

Beet, Lobster & Spinach Risotto

Serves: 4 | Prep: 15 minutes | Cook: 30 minutes

Per serving: 722 CAL | 34.3G FAT | 18.7G SAT FAT | 71.2G CARBS | 8.5G SUGAR | 5.5G FIBER | 29.5G PROTEIN | 2,240MG SODIUM

There is a tendency to think of lobster as a luxury food item, but it offers a wide range of health benefits—it is a good source of omega 3-fatty acids and also of phospherous, zinc, the trace element selenium, and Vitamin B12.

Ingredients

6⅓ cups vegetable broth or chicken broth

2 tablespoons butter

2 tablespoons olive oil

1 small onion, diced

1½ cups risotto rice

½ cup dry white wine

5 small raw beets, grated

1 teaspoon grated horseradish

juice of ⅓ lemon

6 cups baby leaf spinach

8 ounces ready-to-eat lobster meat or crabmeat

1⅓ cups freshly grated Parmesan cheese

salt and pepper, to taste (optional)

⅔ cup crème fraîche or Greek-style yogurt, to serve

1. Bring the broth to a boil in a large saucepan, then simmer over low heat. Meanwhile, heat the butter and oil in a separate large saucepan over medium heat, add the onion, and sauté for 3 minutes. Add the rice and stir to coat with the butter and oil. Cook for an additional 2 minutes. Add the wine and simmer for 2 minutes, or until absorbed.

2. Add the beets and stir well. Add 2 ladles of hot broth to the pan, then cover and cook for 2 minutes, or until absorbed. Stir well and add another ladle of broth. Stir constantly until the broth is absorbed, then add another ladle. Continue adding the broth, one ladle at a time, until it has all been absorbed and the rice is almost cooked.

3. Stir in the horseradish and lemon juice, then add the spinach and season with salt and pepper, if using. Divide among warm bowls, top with the lobster or crabmeat and cheese, and serve immediately, accompanied by the crème fraîche.

Sweet Bell Peppers

The longer you cook bell peppers, the sweeter and softer they will become.

Chicken Peperonata Bowl

Serves: 4 | Prep: 15 minutes | Cook: 35 minutes

Per serving : 571CAL | 9.9G FAT | 2G SAT FAT | 68.6G CARBS | 10.8G SUGAR | 5.9G FIBER | 48.3G PROTEIN | 120MG SODIUM

Bell peppers are rich in capsicum, which has been shown to have antibacterial properties and to reduce triglycerides and LDL cholesterol. They are also rich in vitamins C and A, as well as in iron, potassium, selenium, and magnesium.

Ingredients

2 red bell peppers, seeded and sliced

2 yellow bell peppers, seeded and sliced

1 tablespoon olive oil

2 red onions, peeled and finely sliced

10½ ounces dried penne

4 skinless chicken breasts

2 garlic cloves, crushed

1¼ cups chopped fresh basil

2 tablespoons balsamic vinegar

2 tablespoons fresh Parmesan cheese shavings

salt and pepper, to taste (optional)

1. Put the red bell peppers, yellow bell peppers, and oil into a skillet over medium heat. Cover and cook gently for 15 minutes.

2. Add the onions and cook for an additional 15 minutes.

3. Meanwhile, cook the penne according to the package directions.

4. Preheat a ridged grill pan to hot, add the chicken breasts, and cook for 6–8 minutes on each side, until cooked through.

5. Meanwhile, toss the garlic and basil into the bell pepper mixture, then add the vinegar and cook for 2–3 minutes.

6. Drain the penne and toss into the peperonata. Season with salt and pepper, if using.

7. Slice the chicken breasts diagonally. Divide the penne among four warm bowls. Top with the chicken and some Parmesan cheese shavings.

We know that vegetables are good for us.
they also provide a colorful and versatile
offering for delicious creations on a plate.
Here you'll find new takes on old favorites
and some exotic new spins. Whether it's a
Seaweed Power Bowl or a Veggie Burger Bowl,
Tabbouleh-Stuffed Jalapeños, or Stir-Fried
Brussels Sprouts with Almonds, vegetables are
a constant source of deliciousness.

FRESH BURST

Seaweed Power Bowl

Serves: 4 | Prep: 20 minutes | Cook: none

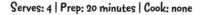

Per serving: 252 CAL | 13.4G FAT | 1.9G SAT FAT | 31G CARBS | 22.2G SUGAR | 6.4G FIBER | 4.8G PROTEIN | 160MG SODIUM

Seaweed is an extraordinary source of a nutrient missing in almost every other food—iodine. This is critically important to maintaining a healthy thyroid. A small serving of seaweed just once a week is recommended.

Ingredients

¼ ounce dried kelp or kombu

½ cucumber

2 oranges

1 red chile, seeded and finely diced

2 carrots, grated

1 large mango, peeled, pitted, and chopped

3 heads of bok choy, chopped

small handful of fresh mint leaves

small handful of fresh cilantro leaves

2 tablespoons chopped salted peanuts

Dressing

3 tablespoons olive oil

grated zest and juice of 1 lime

1 teaspoon honey

1 teaspoon miso paste

1. Put the kelp into a bowl of water and let stand for 10 minutes to rehydrate.

2. Meanwhile, to make the dressing, whisk together the oil, lime zest and juice, honey, and miso paste.

3. Halve the cucumber lengthwise and, using a teaspoon, scoop out and discard the seeds.

4. Peel the oranges and cut them into sections.

5. Coarsely chop the kelp and put into a large bowl with the cucumber, orange sections, chile, carrot, mango, bok choy, and half the mint and cilantro.

6. Pour in the dressing and toss well. Divide among four bowls.

7. Sprinkle each bowl with chopped peanuts and the remaining mint and cilantro.

Why Not Try?

If you can't find dried kelp or kombu, substitute it with nori sheets, which can be served dry, broken into shards, to add an extra crunch to the salad.

Vegetable Rice Bowl

Serves: 4 | Prep: 20 minutes, plus 10 minutes marinating, plus cooling | Cook: 20 minutes

Per serving : 698 CAL | 30.2G FAT | 5G SAT FAT | 81.3G CARBS | 12.6G SUGAR | 4.8G FIBER | 27.4G PROTEIN | 320MG SODIUM

This recipe includes a homemade chili sauce—you can make it as hot as you want. The recipe also works well with shrimp, chicken, or shredded beef.

Ingredients

2–3 red chiles, seeded and finely chopped

3 garlic cloves, crushed

¼ cup white wine vinegar

2 tablespoons sugar

¼ cup sunflower oil

1 tablespoon soy sauce

1 tablespoon sesame oil

1 teaspoon honey

10½ ounces tofu, cut into cubes

1⅓ cups basmati rice or other long-grain rice

1 large carrot, peeled and sliced into thin strips

3 cups sliced cremini mushrooms

½ cup shredded snow peas

2 cups baby spinach leaves

4 eggs

1 tablespoon black sesame seeds

1. Put the chiles, garlic cloves, the vinegar, and sugar into a small saucepan and bring to a boil. Remove from the heat and let cool, then stir in 2 tablespoons of sunflower oil. Set aside.

2. Combine the soy sauce, sesame oil, and honey and put into a nonmetallic bowl with the tofu; let marinate for 10 minutes.

3. Cook the rice according to the package directions. Drain. Meanwhile, heat 1 tablespoon of the remaining sunflower oil in a saucepan, add the carrots and mushrooms, and cook for 4–5 minutes, until soft. Transfer to a plate with a slotted spoon.

4. Put the cooked rice in the pan, then add the marinated tofu, carrots, mushrooms, snow peas, and spinach. Cover and cook for 2–3 minutes.

5. Meanwhile, heat the remaining sunflower oil in a skillet, add the eggs, and cook to your preference. Divide the mixture among four warm bowls. Top each one with a fried egg and spoonful of chili sauce, sprinkle with the sesame seeds, and serve.

Chorizo & Kale Soup

Serves: 6 | Prep: 25 minutes | Cook: 35 minutes

Per serving : 344 CAL | 20.3G FAT | 5.4G SAT FAT | 34.2G CARBS | 5.1G SUGAR | 6.7G FIBER | 11G PROTEIN | 1,320MG SODIUM

This gorgeous, vividly colored soup combines nutrient-packed greens and crispy spiced chorizo.

Ingredients

3 tablespoons olive oil, plus extra for drizzling

1 onion, finely chopped

2 garlic cloves, finely chopped

8 Yukon gold or white round potatoes (about 2 pounds), diced

6⅓ cups vegetable broth

4½ ounces chorizo, thinly sliced

4 cups shredded kale

salt and pepper, to taste (optional)

1. Heat 2 tablespoons of the oil in a large saucepan. Add the onion and garlic and cook over low heat, stirring occasionally, for 5 minutes, until softened. Add the potatoes and cook for an additional 3 minutes.

2. Increase the heat to medium, pour in the broth, and bring to a boil. Reduce the heat, cover, and cook for 10 minutes.

3. Meanwhile, heat the remaining oil in a skillet. Add the chorizo and cook over low heat, turning occasionally, for a few minutes, until the fat runs. Remove with a slotted spoon and drain on paper towels.

4. Remove the pan of soup from the heat and mash the potatoes with a potato masher. Return to the heat, add the kale, and bring back to a boil. Reduce the heat and simmer for 5–6 minutes, until tender.

5. Remove the pan from the heat and mash the potatoes again. Stir in the chorizo, season with salt and pepper, if using, and ladle into warm bowls. Drizzle with a little oil and serve immediately.

Cool Kale

Kale is one of the most nutrient-dense vegetables you can eat. Just a few of its vitamins and minerals include magnesium, potassium, manganese, copper, calcium, and vitamins A, K, C, and B6.

Beautiful Beets

Beets are rich in betaine, a compound
that helps improve digestion and
nutrient absorption, reduce bloating,
calm food intolerances, and control
yeast and bacterial growth. Its
nitrates can also raise "good"
HDL cholesterol, protect against
blood clots, and lower high blood
pressure for up to 24 hours.

Borscht

Serves: 4 | 25–30 minutes, plus standing | Cook: 1¾ hours

Per serving : 358 CAL | 19.4 FAT | 11.8G SAT FAT | 45.5G CARBS | 30.1G SUGAR | 11.4G FIBER | 7.3G PROTEIN | 1,600MG SODIUM

It's hard to beat the magnificent ruby red color of this European soup, particularly favored in Russia, the Ukraine, and Poland.

Ingredients

12 raw beets (about 2¼ pounds)

5 tablespoons butter

2 onions, thinly sliced

3 carrots, thinly sliced

3 celery stalks, thinly sliced

6 tomatoes, peeled, seeded, and chopped

1 tablespoon red wine vinegar

1 tablespoon sugar

2 garlic cloves, finely chopped

1 bouquet garni

5⅓ cups vegetable broth

salt and pepper, to taste (optional)

¼ cup sour cream

2 tablespoons chopped fresh dill, to garnish

1. Peel and shred four of the beets. Melt the butter in a large saucepan. Add the onions and cook over low heat, stirring occasionally, for 5 minutes, until softened. Add the shredded beets, carrots, and celery, and cook, stirring occasionally, for an additional 5 minutes.

2. Increase the heat to medium and add the tomatoes, vinegar, sugar, garlic, and bouquet garni. Season with salt and pepper, if using. Stir well, pour in the broth, and bring to a boil. Reduce the heat, cover, and simmer for 1¼ hours.

3. Meanwhile, peel and shred the remaining beet. Add it and any juices to the pan and simmer for an additional 10 minutes. Remove the pan from the heat and let stand for 10 minutes.

4. Remove and discard the bouquet garni. Ladle the soup into warm bowls and top each with a spoonful of sour cream. Garnish with dill and serve immediately.

Summer Garden Salad

Serves: 4 | Prep: 25 minutes, plus cooling | Cook: 20 minutes

Per serving : 121 CAL | 3.6 FAT | 0.5G SAT FAT | 18.7G CARBS | 11.3G SUGAR | 7.7 FIBER | 5.8G PROTEIN | TRACE SODIUM

A spicy, low-fat tomato dressing makes a wonderful match for green beans and crisp lettuce. This salad is great on its own, or served with sliced and barbecued chicken or fish.

Ingredients

5 cups thinly sliced green beans

2 large tomatoes, diced

2 Boston or other butter lettuce, leaves separated

⅔ cup finely chopped fresh mint

½ cup coarsely snipped fresh chives

Dressing

2 teaspoons olive oil

1 red onion, finely chopped

2 garlic cloves, finely chopped

4 tomatoes, diced

1 teaspoon smoked hot paprika

3 tablespoons sherry vinegar

salt and pepper, to taste (optional)

1. Put the beans into a saucepan of boiling water. Bring back to a boil, then simmer for 3–4 minutes, or until just tender. Drain in a colander, rinse with cold water, then drain again and let cool.

2. To make the dressing, heat the oil in a saucepan over medium–low heat. Add the onion and sauté for 5 minutes, until just beginning to soften. Add the garlic, tomatoes, and paprika, followed by the vinegar, and season with salt and pepper, if using. Cover and simmer for 5 minutes, until the tomatoes are softened and saucy. Transfer to a salad bowl and let cool.

3. Add the beans to the dressing and toss gently together. Add the uncooked tomatoes, lettuce, mint, and chives, toss gently together, then serve.

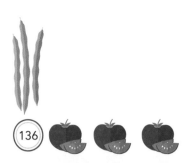

Beets

Not only are beets low in calories, but they are packed full of nutrients that can benefit your health. These include phytonutrients, vitamins (particularly vitamin C), minerals, and antioxidants, which can help protect against breast, colon, and prostate cancers, and reduce LDL, or "bad cholesterol," levels in the blood. They are rich in glutamine, which helps keep the intestinal tract healthy.

Veggie
Burger Bowl

Serves: 4 | Prep: 25 minutes, plus 20 minutes chilling | Cook: 35–40 minutes

Per serving : 534 CAL | 24G FAT | 4G SAT FAT | 66G CARBS | 18.6G SUGAR | 15.8G FIBER | 16.9G PROTEIN | 40MG SODIUM

These burgers are filling and nutritious—and, although you could eat them in a bun, serving them in a bowl on a bed of colorful roasted ratatouille is even better. This dish is full of vitamins, minerals, and fiber, all perfectly balanced to keep you fit and healthy.

Ingredients

2 red bell peppers, seeded and chopped

2 yellow bell peppers, seeded and chopped

2 red onions, cut into wedges

2 zucchini, thickly sliced

3 tablespoons olive oil

1⅓ cups drained and rinsed, canned garbanzo beans

1⅓ cups drained frozen peas, thawed

1⅓ cups frozen corn kernels, thawed

large handful of fresh cilantro (including stems)

¼ teaspoon ground cumin

⅔ cup all-purpose flour

1 tablespoon sunflower seeds

1 tablespoon sesame seeds

salt and pepper, to taste (optional)

Dressing

1 avocado, peeled, pitted, and chopped

1 cup plain yogurt

2 scallions, chopped

1 garlic clove, crushed

1 tablespoon lime juice

salt and pepper, to taste (optional)

1. Preheat the oven to 400°F.

2. Put the red bell peppers, yellow bell peppers, onions, and zucchini into a roasting pan and drizzle with 1 tablespoon of the oil. Roast in the oven for 35–40 minutes, until slightly charred at the edges.

3. Meanwhile, put the garbanzo beans, peas, corn, half the cilantro, the cumin, and ½ cup of the flour into a food processor and process to a thick paste. Add the sunflower seeds and sesame seeds, season with salt and pepper, if using, and process again to mix together.

4. Using wet hands, divide the mixture into four portions and shape each portion into a patty. Dust the patties with the remaining flour and chill in the refrigerator for 20 minutes.

5. Meanwhile to make the dressing, put the avocado, yogurt, scallions, garlic, and lime juice into a small blender and blend until smooth. Season with salt and pepper, if using.

6. Heat the remaining oil in a skillet, add the patties, and cook for 5–6 minutes on each side, until cooked through.

7. Divide the roasted ratatouille among four bowls, top each portion with a patty, then drizzle with the dressing and serve immediately.

Rainbow Salad

Serves: 4 | Prep: 20 minutes | Cook: 6–8 minutes

Per serving : 438 CAL | 32.9G FAT | 10.9G SAT FAT | 23.4G CARBS | 16.6G SUGAR | 4.8G FIBER | 17G PROTEIN | 600MG SODIUM

Eating colorful, fresh food will mean that you will be eating a varied and nutritious diet. Mango, bell peppers, blueberries, and tomatoes are all rich in antioxidants, and nuts and seeds provide the essential fats needed for healthy cell membranes and for your brain.

Ingredients

7 ounces halloumi or Muenster cheese, sliced

1½ cups arugula

1 mango, peeled, pitted, and chopped

12 cherry tomatoes, halved

1 yellow bell pepper, seeded and sliced

10 snow pea pods, shredded

4 scallions, thinly sliced

⅓ cup blueberries

¼ cup sunflower seeds, toasted

¼ cup pumpkin seeds, toasted

¼ cup alfalfa sprouts

Dressing

3 tablespoons olive oil

juice of 1 lemon

1 teaspoon honey

1 teaspoon mustard

1. To make the dressing, whisk together the oil, lemon juice, honey, and mustard.

2. Add the cheese to a dry skillet and cook for 3–4 minutes on each side, until golden.

3. Meanwhile, divide the arugula among four bowls, then top with the mango, tomatoes, yellow bell pepper, snow peas, scallions, and blueberries.

4. Top each serving with slices of cheese and sprinkle with the sunflower and pumpkin seeds and alfalfa sprouts.

5. Drizzle with the dressing and serve immediately.

Why Not Try?

The variations on this salad are endless. Use papaya instead of mango as an aid to digestion, or top the salad with broiled salmon or chicken for extra protein.

Serve It with ...

For a balanced meal, this beautiful coleslaw would be perfect served with broiled fish, such as tuna or mackerel fillets. Or if you are having a summer barbecue, try it with barbecued chicken or chops.

Colorful Coleslaw

Serves: 4 | Prep: 25 minutes | Cook: none

Per serving: 174 CAL | 9.2G FAT | 1.1G SAT FAT | 19.4G CARBS | 10.2G SUGAR | 6G FIBER | 6.1G PROTEIN | 80MG SODIUM

Coleslaw is great served with fish or chicken—and this one is full of color, which means it's also full of nutrients. Cabbage is rich in fiber, bell peppers are rich in antioxidants, and nuts and seeds give you extra essential fats.

Ingredients

¼ cup plain yogurt

½ teaspoon Dijon mustard

juice of 1 lime

½ teaspoon honey

2 teaspoons tahini

1 cup shredded red cabbage

1 cup shredded green cabbage

2 carrots, grated

1 small red onion, thinly sliced

1 red bell pepper, seeded and thinly sliced

1 yellow bell pepper, seeded and thinly sliced

1 fennel bulb, trimmed and shredded

4 radishes, thinly sliced

1 tablespoon chopped fresh basil

1 tablespoon chopped fresh parsley

1 tablespoon chopped fresh mint

3 tablespoons pine nuts, toasted

2 tablespoons hemp seeds, toasted

1. Put the yogurt, mustard, lime juice, honey, and tahini into a large bowl and mix to combine.

2. Add the remaining ingredients and toss well to coat with the dressing.

Sichuan Mixed Vegetables

Serves: 4 | Prep: 20 minutes | Cook: 10 minutes

Per serving : 477 CAL | 14.2G FAT | 2.2G SAT FAT | 76.2G CARBS | 11.9G SUGAR | 7.4G FIBER | 14.1G PROTEIN | 720MG SODIUM

The Sichuan province in Southwest China is characterized by bold flavors and a liberal use of chile and garlic. This recipe follows the same format.

Ingredients

2 tablespoons chili oil

4 garlic cloves, crushed

2-inch piece fresh ginger, grated

4 carrots, cut into thin strips

1 red bell pepper, cut into thin strips

5½ ounces shiitake mushrooms, sliced

2 cups diagonally halved snow peas

3 tablespoons soy sauce

3 tablespoons peanut butter

3⅓ cups bean sprouts

3¾ cups hot cooked rice, to serve

1. Heat the chili oil in a preheated wok and sauté the garlic, ginger, and carrots for 3 minutes. Add the red bell pepper and stir-fry for an additional 2 minutes. Add the mushrooms and snow peas and stir-fry for 1 minute.

2. Mix the soy sauce and peanut butter together in a small bowl until combined. Using a wooden spoon, make a space in the center of the stir-fried vegetables so that the bottom of the wok is visible. Pour in the peanut butter mixture and bring to a boil, stirring constantly, until it starts to thicken. Add the bean sprouts and toss the vegetables to coat thoroughly with the sauce.

3. Transfer to a warm serving dish and serve immediately with freshly cooked rice.

Go for Garlic

Valued for thousands of years as a protector of health, garlic bulbs are a useful antibiotic and can also reduce the risk of heart disease and cancer. Although often used in only small quantities, garlic is rich in powerful sulfur compounds, which also cause its strong odor.

Roasted Vegetable Bowl

Serves: 4 | Prep: 18 minutes | Cook: 35–40 minutes

Per serving : 348 CAL | 28.7G FAT | 3.3G SAT FAT | 21.8G CARBS | 10.2G SUGAR | 7.6G FIBER | 7.9G PROTEIN | 0.1G SALT

Roasting vegetables brings out their flavor; cook them to just char the edges, slightly caramelizing them. This dish includes plenty of color, so it is rich in nutrients. Adding walnuts to your hummus increases your intake of essential fats.

Ingredients

1 yellow zucchini, trimmed and sliced

1 green zucchini, trimmed and sliced

8 thin asparagus spears, trimmed and halved

1 red bell pepper, seeded and chopped

1 yellow bell pepper, seeded and chopped

1 red onion, cut into 8 wedges

1 fennel bulb, trimmed and sliced

¼ cup olive oil

2 teaspoons cumin seeds

¾ cup rinsed and drained, canned garbanzo beans

½ cup walnuts

2 tablespoons lemon juice

2 garlic cloves, crushed

2 tablespoons tahini

3–4 tablespoons water

⅛ teaspoon paprika

½ bunch of watercress or 1¾ cups other peppery greens

4 fresh mint sprigs

salt and pepper, to taste (optional)

1. Preheat the oven to 400°F.

2. Divide the chopped and sliced vegetables between two roasting pans and drizzle each one with 1 tablespoon of the oil and 1 teaspoon of cumin seeds. Toss well to coat the vegetables with the oil. Season with salt and pepper, if using.

3. Roast the vegetables in the preheated oven for 35–40 minutes, until they start to char at the edges.

4. Meanwhile, to make the hummus, put the garbanzo beans and walnuts into a food processor and process until broken down.

5. With the machine running, add the lemon juice and then the garlic, tahini, and remaining oil. Add 3–4 tablespoons of water to loosen, then add the paprika and salt and pepper, if using.

6. Divide the watercress and roasted vegetables among four bowls, then top with a dollop of walnut hummus. Sprinkle with mint sprigs to serve.

Flatbread Pizza with Zucchini Ribbons

Serves: 2 | Prep: 20 minutes | Cook: 10 minutes

Per serving: 592 CAL | 34.4G FAT | 10.7G SAT FAT | 60G CARBS | 3.3G SUGAR | 8.7G FIBER | 15.2G PROTEIN | 2.1G SALT

This fresh, Mediterranean-style lunch with a satisfying crunchy base and fresh vegetable topping is sure to keep hunger pangs at bay.

Ingredients

¼ cup crème fraîche or mascarpone cheese

1 zucchini, shredded into ribbons, using a vegetable peeler

4 cherry tomatoes, quartered

¼ cup ricotta cheese

1 garlic clove, crushed

2 tablespoons olive oil

Pizza Crusts

¾ cup whole wheat all-purpose flour, plus 4 teaspoons for dusting

⅓ cup plus 2 tablespoons quinoa flour

¾ teaspoon baking soda

1 tablespoon olive oil

2 tablespoons warm water

sea salt, to taste (optional)

1. Preheat the oven to 400°F. To make the crusts, put the flours and baking soda into a mixing bowl, season with salt, if using, and stir. Add the oil, then gradually mix in enough of the warm water to make a soft, but not sticky, dough.

2. Lightly dust a work surface with flour. Knead the dough for 2 minutes, until smooth and slightly elastic.

3. Put two large, flat baking sheets into the oven to get hot. Divide the dough into two pieces. Roll out each piece to a circle about ¼-inch thick. Remove the hot baking sheets from the oven and, working quickly, lay the dough on top. Spread the crème fraîche over the dough, then sprinkle with the zucchini and tomatoes. Blob the ricotta cheese in small dollops on top.

4. Bake the pizzas for 7–10 minutes, or until the crust is crispy and slightly puffed up, and the ricotta is tinged golden.

5. Mix the garlic and oil together in a small bowl, and drizzle over the pizzas.

Tabbouleh-Stuffed Jalapeños

Serves: 4 | Prep: 22 minutes | Cook: 10–12 minutes

Per serving: 331 CAL | 18.4G FAT | 2.5G SAT FAT | 40.3G CARBS | 9.5G SUGAR | 15.5G FIBER | 8.6G PROTEIN | 200MG SODIUM

Jalapeño peppers are small in size but can pack a punch with flavor and nutrition. Part of the nightshade family, these little peppers derive their heat from a natural compound called capsicum, known to offer powerful health benefits.

Ingredients

½ cup quinoa

2 cups chopped fresh parsley

2⅓ cups chopped fresh mint

2⅓ cups chopped fresh cilantro

1 preserved lemon, chopped

1 tablespoon chopped walnuts

seeds from 1 pomegranate

24 jalapeño chiles, halved and seeded

2 avocados, peeled, pitted, and sliced

juice of 1 lemon

salt and pepper, to taste (optional)

1. To make tabbouleh stuffing, cook the quinoa according to the package directions. Drain and refresh under cold water, then drain again. Put into a large bowl.

2. Add the parsley, mint, cilantro, preserved lemon, walnuts, and pomegranate seeds and mix thoroughly. Season with salt and pepper, if using.

3. Spoon the tabbouleh into the jalapeños. Top each one with a couple of slices of avocado, then squeeze with the lemon juice to serve.

Asparagus & Zucchini

Asparagus is an anti-inflammatory and contains a fiber that keeps the digestive system healthy. It is also a source of vitamin C, folate, magnesium, potassium, and iron. Zucchini provide immune-system-boosting vitamin C and significant levels of potassium, which help control blood pressure. Zucchini skin has a soluble fiber that slows down digestion, stabilizing blood sugar levels.

Kimchi Tofu Bowl

Serves: 4 | Prep: 20 minutes | Cook: 20–25 minutes

Per serving : 423 CAL | 11.4G FAT | 4.3G SAT FAT | 59.4G CARBS |110G SUGAR | 8.7G FIBER | 18.8G PROTEIN | 480MG SODIUM

Kimchi is a Korean pickle, used to add a sour, tangy flavor to food; it is said to be good for digestion and all-round health. Making kimchi at home can take up to five days, but you can buy it from Korean stores or online.

Ingredients

1¼ cups mixed brown rice, red Carmargue rice, and wild rice

3 cups cold water

3 tablespoons mirin

1 teaspoon soy sauce

2 tablespoons miso paste

7 ounces tofu, cut into triangles

1 tablespoon coconut oil

2 red bell peppers, seeded and sliced

4 scallions, trimmed and sliced

2 zucchini, cut into thick matchsticks

1 carrot, cut into matchsticks

2½ ounces shiitake mushrooms, sliced

½ cup edamame (soybeans)

½ cup bean sprouts

¼ cup kimchi

1. Rinse the rice thoroughly. Put it into a saucepan with the water. Bring to a boil, then cover and simmer gently for 20–25 minutes, or according to package directions, until cooked.

2. Meanwhile, mix together the mirin, soy sauce, and miso paste and put into a nonmetallic bowl. Add the tofu triangles, turning to coat with the marinade, then let marinate for 15–20 minutes.

3. Heat the coconut oil in a wok or large skillet, add the red bell peppers and scallions, and stir-fry for 2–3 minutes, then add the zucchini and carrots and stir-fry for an additional 3–4 minutes.

4. Add the mushrooms, edamame, bean sprouts, tofu, and marinade. Stir-fry for 1 minute, then cover and steam for 2 minutes.

5. Drain the rice and divide among four warm bowls. Top each portion with the stir-fry and 1 tablespoon of kimchi.

Top Up with Tofu

This recipe includes tofu, a good source of vegetarian protein, but you could use strips of chicken or shrimp, if you prefer.

Squash, Kale & Farro Stew

Serves: 6 | Prep: 30 minutes | Cook: 55 minutes

Per serving : 246 CAL | 7.2G FAT | 1.5G SAT FAT | 38.4G CARBS | 9.4G SUGAR | 6.4G FIBER | 9.2G PROTEIN | 440MG SODIUM

This is possibly one of the most colorful stews you could hope to create and eat. It's beneficial to eat from the full range of the vegetable color spectrum— here, we have red tomatoes, orange squash, and green kale.

Ingredients

1 winter squash (about 2¾ pounds), such as kabocha, buttercup, or butternut

2 tablespoons vegetable oil

1 onion, finely chopped

2 teaspoons dried oregano

2 garlic cloves, finely sliced

1⅓ cups canned diced tomatoes

3 cups vegetable broth

¾ cup quick-cooking farro or emmer wheat, rinsed

3¾ cups sliced kale

1½ cups rinsed and drained, canned garbanzo beans

⅓ cup chopped fresh cilantro

juice of 1 lime

salt and pepper, to taste (optional)

1. Cut the squash into quarters, peel, and seed. Cut the flesh into large cubes (you will need about 4½ cups).

2. Heat the oil in a flameproof casserole dish or heavy saucepan. Add the onion and sauté over medium heat for 5 minutes, until translucent. Add the oregano and garlic and sauté for 2 minutes.

3. Add the squash and cook, covered, for 10 minutes.

4. Add the tomatoes, broth, and farro, cover, and bring to a boil. Reduce the heat to a gentle simmer and cook for 20 minutes, stirring occasionally.

5. Add the kale and garbanzo beans. Cook for an additional 15 minutes, or until the kale is just tender.

6. Season with salt and pepper, if using. Stir in the cilantro and lime juice just before serving.

Brussels Boom

Brussels sprouts provide high levels of vitamin C and many other immune-boosting nutrients. They are rich in the sulforaphane compound, which is a detoxifier and has been shown to help the body clear itself of potential carcinogens.

Stir-Fried Brussels Sprouts with Almonds

Serves: 4 | Prep: 20 minutes | Cook: 15 minutes

Per serving: 187 CAL | 13.7G FAT | 1.9G SAT FAT | 14.7G CARBS | 3.3G SUGAR | 5.4G FIBER | 5.5G PROTEIN | 80MG SODIUM

Brussels sprouts are most commonly available in the winter. Here, combined with fresh ginger and almonds, blanched, and then stir-fried, they form the basis of a veritable vegetable power meal.

Ingredients

1 pound Brussels sprouts, tough outer leaves and stems removed

2 tablespoons peanut oil

1 tablespoon toasted sesame oil

1 shallot, finely chopped

1¼-inch piece fresh ginger, finely chopped

1 garlic clove, thinly sliced

3–4 tablespoons chicken broth or vegetable broth

juice of ½ lime

3 tablespoons unskinned almonds (halved lengthwise)

¼ cup chopped fresh cilantro

salt and pepper, to taste (optional)

4 lime wedges, to garnish

1. Bring a large saucepan of water to a boil. Add the Brussels sprouts and blanch for 3 minutes. Drain and rinse under cold running water, then pat dry with paper towels. Slice lengthwise into quarters.

2. Heat a wok or large skillet over medium–high heat. Add the peanut oil and sesame oil. Add the shallot, ginger, and garlic and stir-fry for 1–2 minutes, or until the garlic is just starting to brown.

3. Add the sprouts, broth, and lime juice. Season with salt and pepper, if using, then stir-fry for 2–3 minutes, until the sprouts are beginning to soften. Stir in the almonds and stir-fry for 1–2 minutes, or until the sprouts are tender but still bright green.

4. Stir in the cilantro, garnish with lime wedges, and serve immediately.

Cauliflower, Kale & Garbanzo Bean Bowl

Serves: 4 | Prep: 20 minutes | Cook: 40 minutes

Per serving: 406 CAL | 19.5G FAT | 4.2G SAT FAT | 41.4G CARBS | 10.7G SUGAR | 12.2G FIBER | 19.5G PROTEIN | 360MG SODIUM

Including a variety of spices in your diet can improve health: ginger is considered a cure-all, turmeric is an anti-inflammatory, and cinnamon can be beneficial in helping to control blood sugar. It's time to spice up your life.

Ingredients

1 teaspoon turmeric

1 teaspoon mustard seeds

½ teaspoon cumin seeds

½ teaspoon ground ginger

½ teaspoon ground coriander

½ teaspoon ground cinnamon

1 head of cauliflower, broken into florets

1½ cups rinsed and drained, canned garbanzo beans

2 red onions, thickly sliced

2 tablespoons olive oil

3 cups shredded kale

2 cups fresh whole wheat bread crumbs

3 tablespoons walnuts, chopped

2 tablespoons slivered almonds

⅔ cup freshly grated Parmesan cheese

1. Preheat the oven to 400°F.

2. Dry-fry the turmeric, mustard seeds, cumin seeds, ginger, coriander, and cinnamon in a small skillet for 2 minutes, or until the mustard seeds start to "pop."

3. Put the cauliflower florets, garbanzo beans, and onion slices into a large roasting pan. Sprinkle with the spices and toss well together.

4. Drizzle with the oil and toss again.

5. Roast in the preheated oven for 20 minutes.

6. Stir the kale into the roasted vegetables, and roast for an additional 10 minutes, until the vegetables are tender and slightly charred.

7. Mix together the bread crumbs, walnuts, and almonds and grated cheese and sprinkle the topping over the vegetables. Roast for an additional 5–8 minutes, until golden.

8. Divide among four bowls and serve immediately.

Butternut Squash Bowl

Serves: 4 | Prep: 10 minutes | Cook: 50 minutes

Per serving: 626 CAL | 33.5G FAT | 21.2G SAT FAT | 72.6G CARBS | 9.7G SUGAR | 11.6G FIBER | 16.2G PROTEIN | 40MG SODIUM

Plant-base foods do not include all the essential amino acids that make up protein in one ingredient, but lentils and rice will make a complete protein meal.

Ingredients

2 butternut squash

2 tablespoons olive oil

¾ cup mixed brown rice and wild rice

1 teaspoon coconut oil

4 scallions, trimmed and sliced

1¼-inch piece fresh ginger, grated

1 lemongrass stalk, trimmed and finely sliced

1 tablespoon Thai green curry paste

1⅔ cups canned coconut milk

2 cups cooked green lentils

1½ cups Tuscan kale or black-leaf kale

1 tablespoon sesame seeds

1 tablespoon black sesame seeds

handful of fresh cilantro leaves, to garnish

1. Preheat the oven to 400°F.

2. Halve the squash, scoop out the seeds, and score the flesh with a sharp knife.

3. Place the four squash halves on a baking sheet and drizzle with olive oil. Roast in the preheated oven for 40 minutes. Meanwhile, cook the rice according to the package directions.

4. While the rice is cooking, heat the coconut oil in a skillet. Add the scallions, ginger, and lemongrass and cook for 1 minute, then stir in the curry paste and cook for an additional minute.

5. Add the coconut milk and lentils and bring to a boil. Simmer for 15 minutes.

6. Drain the rice and add to the lentil mixture, with the kale. Simmer for 3–4 minutes.

7. Take the squash out of the oven and divide the lentil-and-rice mixture among the four halves.

8. Sprinkle with the sesame seeds and bake for an additional 10 minutes. Sprinkle with the cilantro leaves and serve.

Pastry Protein

You can use this rice pastry for many different pies, and even quiches. It will keep for up to three days in the refrigerator.

Rice-Crusted Vegetable Pie

Serves: 4 | Prep: 20 minutes | Cook: 55 minutes

Per serving : 378 CAL | 17.9G FAT | 2.9G SAT FAT | 45.6G CARBS | 6.5G SUGAR | 5.2G FIBER | 10.6G PROTEIN | 480MG SODIUM

This is a unique way to make a pie without using pastry—perfect for those people who are trying to avoid wheat and dairy. Plus, the rice adds additional protein to something that would otherwise be heavy in carbohydrates.

Ingredients

1 tablespoon olive oil, for oiling

1 cup long-grain brown rice

2 cups vegetable broth

2 tablespoons sesame seeds, toasted

1 egg, beaten

1 red onion, cut into wedges

1 red bell pepper, seeded and chopped

1 bell yellow pepper, seeded and chopped

1 zucchini, sliced

1 sweet potato, chopped

1 tablespoon olive oil

2 teaspoons cumin seeds

handful of fresh basil leaves, shredded

2 tablespoons walnuts, chopped

2 tablespoons slivered almonds

2 tablespoons freshly grated Parmesan cheese

1. Preheat the oven to 350°F. Lightly oil a 9-inch pie plate.

2. Cook the rice according to the package directions, using the broth instead of water.

3. Transfer the cooked rice to a bowl and mix with the sesame seeds and egg.

4. Press the mixture over the bottom and side of the prepared pan with the back of a spoon. Bake in the preheated oven for 15 minutes.

5. Meanwhile, toss the onion, red bell pepper, yellow bell pepper, zucchini, and sweet potato in a roasting pan with the oil and cumin seeds. Roast for 30 minutes.

6. Remove the vegetables from the oven and stir through the shredded basil leaves. Spoon into the rice crust and return to the oven for 15 minutes.

7. Sprinkle with the walnuts, almonds, and grated cheese and cook for 10 minutes. Serve hot.

Baked Root Vegetable & Rosemary Cake

Serves: 4 | Prep: 30 minutes, plus cooling | Cook: 1 hour

Per serving : 163 CAL | 4.1G FAT | 0.6G SAT FAT | 31.1G CARBS | 9.8G SUGAR | 7.7G FIBER | 3.1G PROTEIN | 120MG SODIUM

An unusual way to serve a selection of vegetables, this unsweetened cake is subtly flavored with rosemary and lemon.

Ingredients

1 tablespoon olive oil, for greasing

3 parsnips, shredded

4 carrots, shredded

2 cups shredded celeriac

1 onion, coarsely grated

2 tablespoons chopped fresh rosemary

3 tablespoons lemon juice

salt and pepper, to taste (optional)

sprigs of fresh rosemary, to garnish

1. Preheat the oven to 375°F. Grease an 8-inch springform cake pan and line with parchment paper.

2. Put the parsnip, carrot, and celeriac into separate, small bowls.

3. Mix together the onion, rosemary, and lemon juice in a small bowl. Add one-third of the onion mixture to each vegetable bowl, season with salt and pepper, if using, and stir to mix evenly.

4. Spoon the parsnips into the prepared pan, spreading evenly and pressing down lightly. Top with the carrots, press lightly, then add the celeriac.

5. Top the cake with a piece of lightly oiled aluminum foil and press down to condense the contents. Tuck the foil over the edges of the pan to seal. Place on a baking sheet and bake in the preheated oven for about 1 hour, or until tender.

6. Remove the foil and turn out the cake onto a warm plate. Let cool for 5 minutes, then slice and serve, garnished with rosemary sprigs.

Beans and grains are the slow superpowers of the nutritional world. They are rich in complex carbohydrates, low in fat, and offer various vitamins, minerals, and antioxidants. They also come in many different shapes and sizes. So continue your journey with a slow burn, with recipes ranging from Green Bean Protein Burst and Lentil, Cumin & Amaranth Patties to a Seed Sprout Buckwheat Bowl and a Multigrain Seed Loaf.

SLOW
RELEASE

Tofu & Sweet Potato Bowl

Serves: 4 | Prep: 15 minutes, plus 30 minutes marinating | Cook: 35–40 minutes

Per serving : 537 CAL | 40.8G FAT | 4.8G SAT FAT | 28.4G CARBS | 11.7G SUGAR | 7.8G FIBER | 22.2G PROTEIN | 280MG SODIUM

Because of their intense color, sweet potatoes are rich in antioxidants— always try to eat these instead of white potatoes, which are just rich in starch. Tofu is a good vegetable protein, but if you would prefer meat or fish, this recipe works perfectly well with both.

Ingredients

1 tablespoon soy sauce

1 tablespoon honey

1 teaspoon cumin seeds

13 ounces tofu, cut into strips

1 sweet potato, chopped

1 red onion, cut into wedges

2 carrots, chopped

1 tablespoon olive oil

¾ cup hazelnuts, toasted

¼ cup extra virgin olive oil

juice of ½ orange

juice of ½ lemon

2 teaspoons sherry vinegar

3½ cups baby spinach leaves

½ cup shredded sugar snap peas

2 tablespoons pumpkin seeds, toasted

1. Preheat the oven to 400°F.

2. Mix together the soy sauce, honey, and cumin seeds and put the tofu into the mixture to marinate for 30 minutes.

3. Meanwhile, put the sweet potato, onion, and carrots into a roasting pan, drizzle with olive oil, and roast in the preheated oven for 35–40 minutes, until tender and slightly charred at the edges.

4. Put the hazelnuts into a food processor and process until they are finely chopped. Put into a bowl with the extra virgin olive oil, orange juice, lemon juice, and vinegar and mix to combine.

5. Preheat a wok until hot, then drain the tofu, discarding the marinade, add the tofu to the wok, and stir-fry for 4–5 minutes.

6. Divide the spinach among four bowls and top with the roasted vegetables and tofu. Sprinkle with the shredded peas and the pumpkin seeds and drizzle with the dressing to serve.

Rainbow Rice & Bean Bowl

Serves: 4 | Prep: 15 minutes | Cook: 20–25 minutes

Per serving: 579 CAL | 24.4G FAT | 3.4G SAT FAT | 77.9G CARBS | 9.6G SUGAR | 14.9G FIBER | 16.6G PROTEIN | 40MG SODIUM

This great salad is bursting with color and can be served warm or cold. Mixing rice and beans will mean a complete protein intake for the meal—perfect for vegetarians.

Ingredients

1¼ cups mixed brown rice and wild rice

1⅔ cups rinsed and drained mixed canned beans, such as kidney beans, pinto beans, and garbanzo beans

1⅓ cups frozen corn kernels, thawed

⅔ cup frozen peas, thawed

1 smalll red onion, finely sliced

⅓ cup chopped pistachio nuts

1 large carrot, peeled and shredded

1 large avocado, sliced

small handful of fresh cilantro leaves, to serve

salt and pepper, to taste (optional)

Dressing

zest and juice of 1 lime

2 tablespoons extra virgin olive oil

1 teaspoon honey

1 red chile, seeded and diced

small handful of fresh mint leaves, chopped

1. Cook the rice according to the package directions.

2. Meanwhile, to make the dressing, whisk together the lime zest and juice, oil, honey, chile, and mint.

3. Drain the rice, put it into a large bowl, and mix in the beans, corn, peas, onion, nuts, and carrot. Stir in the dressing and season with salt and pepper, if using.

4. Divide among four bowls, top with the avocado slices, and sprinkle with cilantro leaves to serve.

Why Not Try?

So many things could be added to this bowl; choose your favorite beans, nuts, and vegetables. You could also add fruits for a change of pace— try chopped apricots or blueberries for added color.

Jerk Turkey Soup

Serves: 4 | Prep: 25–30 minutes| Cook: 40 minutes

Per serving : 240 CAL | 6.7G FAT | 1.3G SAT FAT | 24G CARBS | 8.6G SUGAR | 4.7G FIBER | 22.5G PROTEIN | 600MG SODIUM

This soup has all the flavor of Jamaican jerk spices and seasoning and uses ground spices from the pantry, plus a can of cooked black-eyed peas, fresh tomatoes, and low-fat turkey breast, to make a filling and reviving soup.

Ingredients

1 tablespoon olive oil

1 onion, finely chopped

2 garlic cloves, finely chopped

¾-inch piece fresh ginger, peeled and finely chopped

¼ teaspoon grated nutmeg

½ teaspoon ground allspice

⅛ teaspoon crushed red pepper flakes

2 teaspoons ground cumin

2 teaspoons fresh thyme leaves

4 tomatoes, peeled and coarsely chopped

2½ cups turkey broth

1 tablespoon tomato paste

1 tablespoon packed dark brown sugar

1½ cups rinsed and drained, canned black-eyed peas

10 ounces turkey breast cutlets

2 tablespoons chopped fresh cilantro

salt and pepper, to taste (optional)

1. Heat the oil in a saucepan over medium heat, add the onion, and sauté, stirring, for 5 minutes, until just beginning to brown. Sprinkle with the garlic and ginger, then add the nutmeg, allspice, red pepper flakes, and cumin. Add the thyme and tomatoes and mix together well.

2. Pour in the broth, add the tomato paste, sugar, peas, and turkey cutlets and bring to a boil. Cover and simmer for 30 minutes or until the turkey cutlets are cooked through with no hint of pink juices when cut through the center with a knife. Lift the turkey out of the pan, transfer to a plate, and tear into shreds with two forks.

3. Stir the cilantro into the soup with salt and pepper, if using. Ladle into warm bowls, then top with the shreds of turkey and serve immediately.

Embrace Ginger

The main active compounds in ginger are terpenes and gingerols, which have anticancer properties and have been shown to reduce colon, ovarian, and rectal cancer cells.

Green Bean Protein Burst

Serves: 4 | Prep: 12 minutes | Cook: 15 minutes

Per serving : 516 CAL | 37.9G FAT | 23.7G SAT FAT | 21.9G CARBS | 8G SUGAR | 9.5G FIBER | 27.9G PROTEIN | 480MG SODIUM

**This spicy bean dish is perfect when there is a surplus of beans—
served with spiced tofu it will increase your intake of protein and fiber.**

Ingredients

14 ounces tofu, drained

2 tablespoons soy sauce

2 garlic cloves, crushed

1¼-inch piece fresh ginger, grated

⅛ teaspoon crushed red pepper flakes

1⅓ cups fresh or frozen fava beans

3 cups diagonally sliced green beans

1 tablespoon coconut oil

1 red bell pepper, seeded and chopped

1 teaspoon garam masala

1 teaspoon tomato paste

1⅔ cups coconut milk

⅔ cup frozen edamame (soybeans), thawed

1 tablespoon lime juice

2 tablespoons salted cashew nuts

small handful of fresh cilantro

1. Cut the tofu into cubes and put them into a nonmetallic bowl.

2. Mix together the soy sauce, garlic, ginger, and crushed red pepper flakes and pour over the tofu.

3. Meanwhile, bring a large saucepan of water to a boil, add the fava beans and green beans, and blanch for 4 minutes. Drain.

4. Heat the coconut oil in a wok or large skillet, add the red bell pepper, and stir-fry for 2–3 minutes.

5. Add the garam masala and tomato paste and cook for 1 minute, then pour in the coconut milk. Bring to a boil, then add the fava beans, green beans, and edamame and simmer for 4–5 minutes, until the beans are tender.

6. Add the tofu and lime juice and cook for an additional 2–3 minutes, until the tofu is heated through.

7. Serve in four warm bowls, sprinkled with the cashew nuts and cilantro.

Crunchy Noodle Bean Feast

Serves: 4 | Prep: 20 minutes | Cook: 5 minutes

Per serving: 378 CAL | 5G FAT | 0.6G SAT FAT | 69.9G CARBS | 13.1G SUGAR | 6.5G FIBER | 12.6G PROTEIN | 880MG SODIUM

A bright and colorful summery salad, with loads of textures and crunch. Eating raw food can be beneficial, because some nutrients are lost in cooking. However, not all foods are digestible when raw, so try to maintain a good balance of both.

Ingredients

7 ounces vermicelli noodles

1½ cups drained, canned lima beans

1 large carrot, peeled and cut into julienne strips

1 red chile, seeded and finely diced

⅓ cup shredded snow peas

¼ cucumber, cut into julienne strips

4 baby corn, halved lengthwise

2 tablespoons cashew nuts

¾ cup bean sprouts

large handful of fresh mint leaves

large handful of cilantro leaves

large handful of Thai basil leaves

2 tablespoons sesame seeds, toasted

Dressing

2 tablespoons packed brown sugar

2 tablespoons Thai fish sauce

juice of 2 limes

1 garlic clove, crushed

1. Cook the noodles according to the package directions. Drain and put into a bowl.

2. To make the dressing, put the sugar, fish sauce, and lime juice into a small bowl and stir until the sugar has dissolved. Stir in the garlic.

3. Add all the remaining ingredients apart from the toasted sesame seeds to the noodles, pour in the dressing, and toss together well.

4. Serve in four bowls, sprinkled with the toasted sesame seeds.

Lentils & Amaranth

Lentils are a rich source of fiber, which helps protect against cancer and cardiovascular disease. They are also rich in the B vitamins, folate, and all major minerals, particularly iron and zinc. Amaranth is a grain with a high protein content, encouraging growth and the creation of new cells. It contains a peptide that can improve the immune system and reduce inflammation.

Minted Fava Bean Bruschetta

Serves: 4 | Prep: 15 minutes | Cook: 15 minutes

Per serving : 546 CAL | 25.2G FAT | 8.9G SAT FAT | 55.5G CARBS | 6.5G SUGAR | 8.7G FIBER | 22.6G PROTEIN | 760MG SODIUM

Fava beans are a great source of protein and fiber as well as being rich in both folate and the B vitamins, needed for nerve and cell development as well as cognitive function and energy.

Ingredients

2⅔ cups shelled fava beans

¼ cup extra virgin olive oil

juice of 1 lemon

handful of mint leaves, chopped

8 slices sourdough bread

2 garlic cloves, peeled

¾ cup crumbled feta cheese

2 tablespoons pumpkin seeds, toasted

salt and pepper, to taste (optional)

1. Bring a large saucepan of water to a boil. Add the fava beans and cook for 3 minutes. Drain, refresh under cold water, and drain again. Remove the outer skin of the beans, if desired.

2. Use a fork to coarsely mash the beans with 3 tablespoons of the oil and the lemon juice, then stir through the mint. Season with salt and pepper, if using.

3. Heat a ridged grill pan and cook the bread slices on both sides. Rub both sides of the bread with the garlic cloves.

4. Top each slice of bread with the fava bean mixture, followed by the cheese, then sprinkle with the pumpkin seeds and drizzle with the remaining oil.

Lentil, Cumin & Amaranth Patties

Serves: 4 | Prep: 25 minutes, plus 20 minutes chilling | Cook: 20 minutes

Per serving : 553 CAL | 19.1G FAT | 3.4G SAT FAT | 73.4G CARBS | 4G SUGAR | 10.5G FIBER | 24.4G PROTEIN | 80MG SODIUM

Amaranth is a gluten-free seed with a high protein content and beneficial health properties, such as reducing inflammation and helping in bone development. It is also good for digestive health, because it is rich in fiber.

Ingredients

1 cup red lentils

1 cup amaranth

1 sweet potato, chopped

1 teaspoon cumin seeds, toasted

4 scallions, trimmed and diced

1 tablespoon sesame seeds

2 tablespoons whole wheat bread crumbs

small handful of fresh cilantro leaves, chopped

3 tablespoons olive oil

12 quail eggs

salt and pepper, to taste (optional)

1. Put the lentils and amaranth into a saucepan and cover with water. Bring to a boil over high heat, then reduce the heat and simmer for 15 minutes, until swollen and cooked. Drain well.

2. Meanwhile, steam the sweet potato for 10 minutes, until tender.

3. Put the sweet potato, lentils, amaranth, cumin seeds, scallions, sesame seeds, bread crumbs, and cilantro into a large bowl and mix together. Season with salt and pepper, if using.

4. Wet your hands and shape the mixture into 12 patties. Place on a plate or tray and chill in the refrigerator for 20 minutes.

5. Heat 2 tablespoons of the oil in a skillet, then add the patties and cook for 2–3 minutes on each side, until golden.

6. Meanwhile, heat the remaining oil in a separate skillet and fry the eggs.

7. Top each patty with an egg and serve immediately.

Quick Fix

If your mixture is too wet and doesn't
seem to be coming together, just add
some more bread crumbs.

Beet Falafel
with Pita Bread

Serves: 4 | Prep: 30–35 minutes, plus rising | Cook: 35–45 minutes

Per serving : 483 CAL | 14.7G FAT | 2.6G SAT FAT | 69.1G CARBS | 7.5G SUGAR | 7.5G FIBER | 17.6G PROTEIN | 1,120MG SODIUM

Sweet, earthy, and tender to the taste, beets are a sublime ingredient to combine with falafel, keeping them moist. Beets also contain nitrate, which lowers blood pressure and may help to fight heart disease.

Ingredients

4 teaspoons whole wheat flour, for dusting

1 quantity kneaded and risen pizza crust dough made with 1 teaspoon coarsely crushed cumin seeds added with the yeast

3 cups rinsed and drained, canned garbanzo beans

1 red onion, finely chopped

2 garlic cloves, thinly sliced

1 teaspoon cumin seeds, coarsely crushed

1 teaspoon sumac seeds

1 teaspoon baking powder

3 beets, peeled and shredded

3 tablespoons virgin olive oil, for brushing

salt and pepper, to taste (optional)

lettuce leaves, shredded, to serve (optional)

Tzatziki

½ cucumber, halved, seeded, and finely chopped

⅔ cup plain yogurt

2 tablespoons finely chopped fresh mint

1. Preheat the oven to 450°F. To make the pita breads, lightly dust a work surface with flour. Knead the dough, then cut into four pieces and roll out each piece into an oval. Let rise for 10 minutes.

2. Lightly flour two baking sheets, then put them in the oven for 5 minutes. Add the breads to the hot baking sheets and bake for 5–10 minutes, or until lightly browned. Wrap in a clean dish towel to keep them soft.

3. Meanwhile, put the garbanzo beans into a food processor and process them, in small batches, to a coarse paste. Transfer to a bowl. Add the onion, garlic, cumin, sumac, baking powder, and beets. Season with salt and pepper, if using, then mix.

4. Roll the mixture into 20 balls. Brush a large roasting pan with a little oil, then put it in the oven for 5 minutes. Add the falafel and brush generously with more oil. Roast the falafel for 20–25 minutes, turning, until browned and cooked through.

5. Meanwhile, to make the tzatziki, put the cucumber, yogurt, and mint into a bowl, season with salt and pepper, and mix well. To serve, halve the warm pita breads, spoon in the shredded lettuce, if using, tzatziki, and falafel, and serve.

Green Farro Salad with Feta

Serves: 4 | Prep: 20 minutes | Cook: 15 minutes

Per serving : 525 CAL | 33G FAT | 7.1G SAT FAT | 45.7G CARBS | 3.1G SUGAR | 5.3G FIBER | 11.5G PROTEIN | 480MG SODIUM

A favorite in Italy, sweet and chewy farro makes a stylish salad with summery green vegetables and herbs, tangy feta cheese, and a zesty lemon-oil dressing. The salad is just as suitable for a party buffet as it is for a summer lunch.

Ingredients

1¼ cups quick-cooking farro or emmer wheat, rinsed

½ teaspoon salt

⅓ cup fresh peas

5 scallions, some green included, thinly sliced

½ zucchini, shredded

⅔ cup shredded baby spinach

¼ cup chopped fresh mint leaves

¼ cup chopped fresh flat-leaf parsley

3 ounces vegetarian feta cheese, cubed

1 teaspoon sumac or paprika, for sprinkling

2 tablespoons extra virgin olive oil, for drizzling

Dressing

2 tablespoons lemon juice

⅓ cup extra virgin olive oil

salt and pepper, to taste (optional)

1. Put the farro and salt into a saucepan with water to cover. Bring to a boil, then reduce the heat, cover, and simmer for 10 minutes, until tender but still chewy. Drain, then spread out on a tray to cool slightly. Transfer to a serving bowl while still lukewarm.

2. To make the dressing, combine the lemon juice with salt and pepper, if using, in a small bowl. Whisk in the oil. Pour it over the farro and mix gently.

3. Stir in the peas, scallions, zucchini, spinach, mint, and parsley. Let stand at room temperature for 30 minutes.

4. Divide the mixture among four plates. Arrange the cheese on top, sprinkle with a little sumac, and drizzle with oil. Serve immediately.

Dress It Up

Make double or triple the quantity
of dressing, then you can store
the remainder in a screw-top jar
in the refrigerator.

Lentil, Grape & Feta Salad

Serves: 4 | Prep: 16 minutes | Cook: none

Per serving: 475 CAL | 32.8G FAT | 7.5G SAT FAT | 35.1G CARBS | 13.4G SUGAR | 12.5G FIBER | 16G PROTEIN | 320MG SODIUM

This is a fabulous combination—creamy feta cheese with crunchy nuts and sweet grapes, topped with a citrus and herb dressing.

Ingredients

1 romaine lettuce, thickly shredded

1 cup arugula leaves

⅓ cup seedless red grapes

⅓ cup seedless white grapes

1½ cups cooked green lentils

4 scallions, trimmed and sliced

1 red bell pepper, seeded and thinly sliced

⅔ cup pecans, toasted

¾ cup crumbled feta cheese

Dressing

3 tablespoons extra virgin olive oil

1 teaspoon walnut oil

1 teaspoon raspberry vinegar

juice of ½ lemon

2 teaspoons maple syrup

1 teaspoon whole-grain mustard

½ garlic clove, crushed

2 teaspoons chopped fresh mint

2 teaspoons chopped fresh parsley

salt and pepper, to taste (optional)

1. To make the dressing, whisk together the olive oil, walnut oil, vinegar, lemon juice, maple syrup, mustard, garlic, mint, and parsley. Season with salt and pepper, if using.

2. Divide the lettuce and arugula among four large shallow bowls.

3. Halve the red grapes and white grapes. Mix together the lentils, scallions, red grapes, white grapes, and red bell pepper and spoon the mixture over the lettuce and arugula.

4. Chop the pecans, then sprinkle the nuts and cheese over the salad. Drizzle with the dressing and serve immediately.

Seed Sprout Buckwheat Bowl

Serves: 4 | Prep: 10 minutes, plus chilling | Cook: 20 minutes

Per serving : 300 CAL | 10.1G FAT | 0.8G SAT FAT | 49.3G CARBS | 15.8G SUGAR | 10.5G FIBER | 9G PROTEIN | 360MG SODIUM

Seed sprouts and beans make a wonderful addition to a healthy salad at any time of year, while buckwheat adds fiber and a superb nutty flavor.

Ingredients

4 carrots, cut into quarters lengthwise

2⅔ tablespoons extra virgin canola oil

1½ tablespoons maple syrup

⅔ cup kasha (roasted buckwheat groats)

2 cups mixed seed sprouts (such as adzuki beans, alfalfa, radish, and lentil)

¼ cucumber, diced

2 celery stalks, diced

1 red-skinned apple, diced

4 scallions, diced

⅓ cup cooked small peas

juice of 1 orange

juice of ½ lemon

½ teaspoon sea salt

½ teaspoon pepper

½ cup pea shoots

1. Preheat the oven to 375°F.

2. Toss the carrots in 1½ teaspoons of the oil and 1½ teaspoons of the maple syrup. Roast in the preheated oven for 20 minutes, or until golden and just tender. Let cool.

3. Meanwhile, pour the kasha into ¾ cup of boiling water in a large saucepan. Stir and bring to a boil, then reduce to a simmer, put a lid on, and cook for 10 minutes, or according to package directions, until the groats are cooked. Turn off the heat and let the pan stand on the stove for a few minutes with the lid on, then transfer to a serving bowl and let cool.

4. Mix the cooled kasha with the seed sprouts, cucumber, celery, apple, scallions, and peas.

5. Combine the remaining canola oil and maple syrup with the orange and lemon juices and salt and pepper in a small bowl. Stir this dressing into the buckwheat mixture. Top with the roasted carrots and pea shoots, then serve in individual serving bowls.

Tofu Steak with Fennel & Orange

Serves: 4 | Prep: 25 minutes | Cook: 6–8 minutes

Per serving : 175 CAL | 8.7G FAT | 1.1G SAT FAT | 15.1G CARBS | 8.2G SUGAR | 5.2G FIBER | 10.5G PROTEIN | 120MG SODIUM

Tofu is easy to infuse with spicy flavors, so it is ideal for using with hot spices, such as Moroccan harissa or Cajun seasoning.

Ingredients

12 ounces extra firm tofu, drained

1 tablespoon harissa paste

2 teaspoons extra virgin olive oil

1 large orange

1 fennel bulb, thinly sliced

1 small red onion, thinly sliced

8 pitted black ripe olives, halved

1 tablespoon chopped fresh mint, to garnish

1. Preheat the broiler to high. Place the tofu on a clean dish towel and press lightly to remove any excess moisture.

2. Cut the tofu into four thick triangles. Mix the harissa with the oil. Brush this mixture over the tofu.

3. Lift the tofu steaks onto a baking sheet and cook under the preheated broiler for 6–8 minutes, turning once, until golden brown.

4. Meanwhile, use a sharp knife to cut all the rind and white pith from the orange and carefully remove the sections from the membranes, catching the juice in a bowl.

5. Put the orange sections, fennel, onion, and olives into bowl. Mix thoroughly to combine and then divide the mixture among four serving plates.

6. Place the tofu steaks on top, drizzle with the reserved orange juice, and garnish with chopped fresh mint to serve.

Couscous with Cherry Tomatoes & Pine Nuts

Serves: 4 | Prep: 25 minutes, plus standing | Cook: 7–8 minutes

Per serving : 374 CAL | 23.2G FAT | 7.1G SAT FAT | 31.8G CARBS | 4.4G SUGAR | 4.1G FIBER | 11.3G PROTEIN | 320MG SODIUM

Couscous, which is a form of wheat, provides you with a good source of lean, vegetarian protein to support healthy skin, muscles, organs, and other body tissue. An average serving of couscous has less than 0.5 grams of fat.

Ingredients

2 cups cherry tomatoes

3 tablespoons olive oil

¾ cup couscous

1 cup boiling water

¼ cup pine nuts, toasted

⅓ cup coarsely chopped fresh mint

finely grated zest of 1 lemon

1½ teaspoons lemon juice

salt and pepper, to taste (optional)

4 cups torn crisp green lettuce and 1 cup crumbled feta cheese, to serve

1. Preheat the oven to 450°F. Put the tomatoes and 1 tablespoon of the oil into an ovenproof dish. Toss together, then roast for 7–8 minutes in the preheated oven until the tomatoes are soft and the skins have burst. Let stand for 5 minutes.

2. Put the couscous into a heatproof bowl. Pour over the boiling water, cover, and let stand for 8–10 minutes, or according to package directions, until soft and the liquid has been absorbed. Fluff up the couscous with a fork. Add the tomatoes and their juices, the pine nuts, mint, lemon zest, lemon juice, and the remaining oil. Season with salt and pepper, if using, then gently toss together.

3. Serve the couscous warm or cold, with a green salad and some feta cheese.

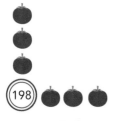

Loaded Sweet Potatoes

Serves: 4 | Prep: 20–25 minutes | Cook: 50–55 minutes

Per serving: 257 CAL | 4.2G FAT | 0.5G SAT FAT | 47.8G CARBS | 9.8G SUGAR | 8.1G FIBER | 8.4G PROTEIN | 360MG SODIUM

This veggy version of a stuffed baked potato is topped with Middle Eastern-spiced garbanzo beans and tomatoes for a light but mighty refueling snack.

Ingredients

4 small sweet potatoes, scrubbed

1 tablespoon olive oil

1 small onion, chopped

1 garlic clove, finely chopped

1 teaspoon ground coriander

½ teaspoon ground cumin

2 tomatoes, peeled and diced

2 teaspoons tomato paste

¾ cup rinsed and drained, canned garbanzo beans

¼ cup chopped fresh cilantro

½ cup fat-free Greek-style yogurt

sea salt and pepper, to taste (optional)

1. Preheat the oven to 375°F. Prick the potatoes with a fork, put them on a baking sheet, and bake in the preheated oven for 45–50 minutes, or until they feel soft when squeezed.

2. Meanwhile, heat the oil in a small skillet, add the onion, and sauté over medium heat for 4–5 minutes, until soft. Stir in the garlic, ground coriander, and cumin, and cook for an additional minute.

3. Mix in the tomatoes, tomato paste, and garbanzo beans, then season with a little salt and pepper, if using. Cover and cook for 10 minutes, then remove from the heat and set aside.

4. Transfer the potatoes to a serving plate, halve each along its length and open out slightly. Reheat the garbanzo beans and spoon them over the potatoes. Mix half the fresh cilantro into the yogurt and spoon it over the garbanzo beans. Sprinkle with the remaining fresh cilantro and serve immediately.

Pumpkin Seeds

A nutritious and easily portable snack,
even in small servings pumpkin seeds
provide a significant amount of minerals,
especially zinc and iron. They also help boost
the immune system, improve fertility,
and contain sterols linked with protection
against hormone-base cancers. They are
a good source of heart-healthy and
anti-inflammatory nutrients.

Cauliflower Flatbreads

Makes: 8 | Prep: 45 minutes, plus cooling and resting | Cook: 30–45 minutes

Per serving: 379 CAL | 20.8G FAT | 11G SAT FAT | 43.1G CARBS | 2.5G SUGAR | 5.2G FIBER | 7.8G PROTEIN | 1,360MG SODIUM

These tasty flatbreads are stuffed with a spiced potato-and-cauliflower mixture. They are delicious eaten with yogurt or a minted yogurt dip.

Ingredients

1¾ cups plus 2 tablespoons whole wheat flour

¾ cup all-purpose flour, plus 4 teaspoons for dusting

1 teaspoon freshly ground cardamom seeds

2 teaspoons salt

1 cup lukewarm buttermilk

1¼ sticks plus 1 tablespoon butter, melted

Filling

2 tablespoons vegetable oil

2 teaspoons cumin seeds

1 tablespoon hot curry powder

4 garlic cloves, crushed

2 teaspoons finely grated fresh ginger

1 cup finely chopped cauliflower florets

2 teaspoons salt

2 potatoes, boiled, peeled, and coarsely mashed

⅓ cup finely chopped fresh cilantro

1. To make the filling, heat the oil in a large skillet over medium heat. Add the cumin seeds, curry powder, garlic, ginger, and cauliflower and stir-fry for 8–10 minutes. Add the salt and potatoes and stir well to mix evenly. Remove from the heat and stir in the cilantro. Let cool.

2. Sift together the whole wheat flour, all-purpose flour, cardamom seeds, and salt into a large bowl, tipping in any bran remaining in the sifter. Make a well in the center and pour in the buttermilk and 2 tablespoons of melted butter. Work into the flour mixture to make a soft dough. Knead on a floured surface for 10 minutes. Shape into a ball and put into a large bowl, cover with a damp cloth, and rest for 20 minutes. Divide the dough into eight balls, then roll out each ball into a 6-inch circle.

3. Place a little of the filling in the center of each circle and fold up the edges of the dough into the center to enclose the filling. Press down lightly and roll out with a rolling pin to a diameter of 6 inches. Repeat with the remaining dough and filling.

4. Heat a cast-iron, flat griddle pan or nonstick, heavy skillet over medium heat. Brush each flatbread with a little of the remaining melted butter. Brush the pan with a little melted butter. Put a flatbread on the pan and cook for 1–2 minutes, pressing down with a spatula. Turn over, brush with a little more butter, and cook for an additional 1–2 minutes, or until flecked with light brown spots. Remove from the pan, transfer to a plate, cover with aluminum foil, and keep warm while you cook the remaining flatbreads. Serve warm.

Multigrain Seed Loaf

Serves: 12 | Prep: 20 minutes, plus 1 hour soaking | Cook: 1 hour 10 minutes–1 hour 15 minutes

Per serving : 464 CAL | 32.6G FAT | 12.6G SAT FAT | 34.1G CARBS | 9.3G SUGAR | 8.6G FIBER | 13.1G PROTEIN | TRACE SODIUM

This densely packed loaf is bursting with fiber, protein, and essential fats, as well as loads of vitamins and minerals. It will certainly fill you up with just one slice. It's perfect topped with avocado or chia preserves.

Ingredients

1 tablespoon sunflower oil, for oiling

3½ tablespoons chia seeds

⅓ cup chopped dates

1 cup water

⅔ cup sunflower seeds

⅔ cup pumpkin seeds

½ cup slivered almonds

1 egg

½ cup ground almonds (almond meal)

1 cup quinoa flakes

2 cups rolled oats

¾ cup plus 2 tablespoons ground flaxseed (flaxseed meal)

⅓ cup maple syrup

⅔ cup coconut oil, melted

1. Grease and line the bottom of a 9 x 5 x 3-inch loaf pan with parchment paper.

2. Put the chia seeds and dates into a large bowl and pour in 1 cup water. Let stand.

3. In a dry skillet, toast the sunflower seeds, pumpkin seeds, and slivered almonds until lightly golden.

4. Put the chia seeds, dates, and water into a food processor with the egg and blend until creamy. Pour the mixture back into the bowl with the remaining ingredients and mix together really well.

5. Spoon into the loaf pan, pressing the batter down thoroughly. Cover with a cloth and let stand for 1 hour.

6. Preheat the oven to 325°F.

7. Bake the loaf for 1 hour. Let cool completely in the pan.

8. Store in an airtight container.

Nuts and Flakes

You can use whatever nuts and flakes
you prefer, as long as you keep the
quantities similar so that the loaf
holds together.

Kale, Shallot & Blue Cheese Biscuits

Makes 10–12 | Prep: 40 minutes, plus cooling | Cook: 25–30 minutes

Per serving: 201 CAL | 11.4G FAT | 5.7G SAT FAT | 19.5G CARBS | 1.8G SUGAR | 2.9G FIBER | 7.2G PROTEIN | 360MG SODIUM

Kale makes a hearty addition to a biscuit mix. Shallots add a little sweetness and moisture, while blue cheese enriches the flavor. Serve freshly baked and lavishly spread with unsalted butter.

Ingredients

12 ounces kale, trimmed
2 tablespoons vegetable oil
2 small shallots, finely chopped
2 cups whole wheat flour
2 teaspoons sugar
2 teaspoons baking powder
½ teaspoon baking soda
¼ teaspoon salt
¼ teaspoon pepper
4½ tablespoons chilled butter, diced
1 cup crumbled blue cheese
1 egg, lightly beaten
about ⅔ cup buttermilk
4 teaspoons all-purpose flour, for dusting
1 egg yolk
1 tablespoon milk
unsalted butter, to serve (optional)

1. Preheat the oven to 400°F. Line a baking sheet with a nonstick parchment paper. Put the kale into the top of a steamer and steam for 7–10 minutes, until tender. Remove from the heat and let cool. Finely chop, then squeeze with your hands to remove as much liquid as possible.

2. Meanwhile, heat the oil in a small skillet over medium heat. Add the shallots and gently sauté for about 5 minutes, until soft. Remove from the heat and let cool.

3. Put the flour, sugar, baking powder, baking soda, salt ,and pepper into the bowl of a food processor and pulse briefly. Add the butter and pulse a few more times until crumbly. Add the shallots, kale, and ½ cup of the cheese. Pulse again to mix. Pour in the beaten egg and ½ cup of the buttermilk. Pulse briefly to a soft, sticky dough. Add more buttermilk if the mixture is dry.

4. Turn out the dough onto a well-floured pastry board. Use a rolling pin to lightly roll out the dough to a ¾-inch thick circle. Using a 2½-inch cutter, cut out 10–12 circles, or cut out triangles, using a sharp knife. Arrange on the prepared baking sheet.

5. Mix the egg yolk with the milk and brush over the biscuit tops. Sprinkle with the remaining cheese. Bake in the middle of the oven for 15–18 minutes, or until well risen and the tip of a knife inserted into the center of a biscuit comes out clean.

6. Slice the biscuits and spread with butter, if using.

It's time for something sweet. But nutrition
is still at the top of the agenda! You'll find
ingredients here that include goji and acai
berries, pineapple, mango, figs, nuts, flaxseed,
chia seeds, almond milk, and cacao. So for your
power finale choose from recipes ranging from
Fig & Oat Bites to Zucchini Loaf Cake and
an Acai Power Bowl to a Healthy Fruit & Nut
Bowl. Yes, power can be sweet, too.

SWEET FIX

Flaxseed Biscotti

Makes: 20–24 biscotti | Prep: 10 minutes | Cook: 40–45 minutes

Per serving : 82 CAL | 2.2G FAT | 0.5G SAT FAT | 13.5G CARBS | 5.1G SUGAR | 1.1G FIBER | 2.1G PROTEIN | 40MG SODIUM

These sweet, crunchy cookies are perfect for serving with coffee. The addition of flaxseed increases the essential fat and fiber content, while cinnamon is good for controlling sugar cravings and blood sugar.

Ingredients

2 eggs

⅓ cup sugar

1⅓ cups all-purpose flour, plus ¼ cup for dusting

¼ cup ground flaxseed (flaxseed meal)

2 tablespoons whole flaxseed

½ teaspoon baking soda

¼ teaspoon ground cinnamon

1 ounce semisweet chocolate, chopped

2 tablespoons chopped pistachio nuts

2 tablespoons dried cranberries

1. Preheat the oven to 350°F. Line a baking sheet with parchment paper. Whisk together the eggs and sugar until light and fluffy.

2. Sift the flour into a bowl and stir in the ground flaxseed, whole flaxseed, baking soda, cinnamon, chocolate, pistachio nuts, and cranberries.

3. Pour the egg mixture into the dry ingredients and mix to a soft dough. Turn out onto a floured surface and shape into a 9½-inch log.

4. Place the dough on the prepared baking sheet and press a little to flatten to a height of 1¼ inches. Bake in the preheated oven for 30 minutes.

5. Remove from the oven and slide onto a cutting board. Reduce the oven temperature to 325°F. Cut the loaf into ½-inch-thick slices and return to the baking sheet, cut side up.

6. Bake for 10–15 minutes, until crisp, then transfer to a wire rack and let cool completely. The biscotti will keep in a sealed container for up to three weeks.

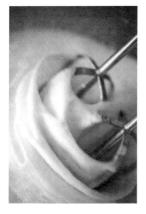

Goji & Mango Popcorn Slices

Makes: 12 | Prep: 25 minutes, plus chilling | Cook: 6–8 minutes

Per slice : 195 CAL | 13.8G FAT | 5.4G SAT FAT | 13.3G CARBS | 7.5G SUGAR | 2.2G FIBER | 4.5G PROTEIN | 40MG SODIUM

This version of "icebox cake" uses mineral-boosting dried fruit and seeds for a nutrient-dense, energy-packed treat.

Ingredients

1 tablespoon light olive oil

3 tablespoons popping corn

⅓ cup chunky peanut butter

2 tablespoons coconut oil

2 tablespoons maple syrup

⅓ cup whole or low-fat milk

3½ ounces bittersweet chocolate, broken into pieces

¼ cup coarsely chopped goji berries

3 tablespoons finely chopped dried mango

3 tablespoons coarsely chopped pistachio nuts

1½ tablespoons sunflower seeds

1½ tablespoons pumpkin seeds

1. Line an 8-inch shallow square cake pan with a sheet of nonstick parchment paper.

2. Heat the olive oil in a skillet, then add the corn, cover with a lid, and cook over medium heat for 3–4 minutes, shaking the pan occasionally, until all the corn has popped. Transfer to a bowl, discarding any kernels that haven't popped, and wipe out the pan with paper towels.

3. Add the peanut butter, coconut oil, maple syrup, and milk, then heat gently for 2–3 minutes, stirring until smooth. Remove from the heat, add the chocolate, and set aside for 4–5 minutes, until the chocolate has melted.

4. Add the popcorn to the chocolate mix and lightly stir together. Transfer to the prepared pan, press down flat with the back of a fork, then sprinkle with the goji berries, mango, pistachios, and sunflower and pumpkin seeds. Press the topping into the soft chocolate mix, then chill in the refrigerator for 2 hours, until firmly set.

5. Lift the chocolate mixture out of the pan, place on a cutting board, peel away and reserve the paper, then cut the "cake" into 12 pieces. Pack into a plastic container, layering with the reserved paper. Keep in the refrigerator for up to four days.

Fig & Oat Bites

Makes: 25 | Prep: 20–25 minutes, plus chilling | Cook: 20 minutes

Per square : 93 CAL | 2.4G FAT | 1.5G SAT FAT | 17.5G CARBS | 9G SUGAR | 2.8G FIBER | 1.7G PROTEIN | TRACE SODIUM

The goodness of whole-grain oats paired with fiber-rich dried figs creates these scrumptious nuggets of goodness that contain no added sugar or salt. A sprinkling of chia seeds and spices adds a boost to their feel-good factor.

Ingredients

2¼ cups soft dried figs (about 1 pound)

3 tablespoons coconut oil, at room temperature

⅓ teaspoon ground ginger

⅓ teaspoon ground cinnamon

juice of 1 large orange

2¼ cups rolled oats

1 tablespoon chia seeds

1. Preheat the oven to 350°F. Line a 9-inch square baking pan with parchment paper.

2. Put the dried figs, coconut oil, ginger, and cinnamon into a food processor and pulse until coarsely chopped. Add the orange juice and oats and pulse again until the mixture just comes together. If a little dry, add a touch more orange juice; if a little wet, stir through a few more oats. Add the chia seeds and pulse again briefly.

3. Spoon the batter into the prepared baking pan. Use the back of a greased spatula to push the mixture to the corners and spread it evenly.

4. Bake in the preheated oven for 20 minutes. Remove from the oven and, using a sharp knife, cut into 25 small squares. Let cool completely on a wire rack and then serve.

Zucchini Loaf Cake

Serves: 10 | Prep: 25 minutes | Cook: 1 hour

Per serving : 237 CAL | 21.9G FAT | 6.5G SAT FAT | 5.3G CARBS | 2.2G SUGAR | 2.4G FIBER | 7.2G PROTEIN | 240MG SODIUM

Zucchini cake is just as delicious as carrot cake. It's supermoist, with a frosting that adds a creamy and fresh flavor.

Ingredients

1¾ cups ground almonds (almond meal)

½ teaspoon baking powder

⅛ teaspoon baking soda

3 tablespoons stevia

⅓ cup chopped mixed nuts

3½ tablespoons butter

2 extra-large eggs, beaten

1 teaspoon vanilla extract

1¾ cups shredded zucchini

Frosting

1 cup cream cheese

1 tablespoon stevia

finely grated zest and juice of ¼ lemon

1. Preheat the oven to 325°F. Line a nonstick 8½ x 4½ x 2½-inch loaf pan with parchment paper.

2. Put the ground almonds, baking powder, baking soda, stevia, and half the nuts into a large bowl and stir well.

3. Melt the butter in a small saucepan over medium–low heat. Pour it onto the dry ingredients. Add the eggs, vanilla, and zucchini, and mix well.

4. Spoon the batter into the prepared pan and spread it into an even layer. Bake for 55–60 minutes, or until well risen and a toothpick comes out clean when inserted into the center of the cake. Let cool for 15 minutes, then remove from the pan, peel off the parchment paper, and transfer to a wire rack.

5. To make the frosting, put the cream cheese and stevia into a large bowl and beat until light and airy. Add the lemon zest and juice, and beat again briefly. Using a spatula, spread the frosting over the top of the cake. Decorate with the remaining nuts and serve.

Brazil Burst

Brazil nuts are actually seeds rather than nuts. They are a rich dietary source of selenium, a vital mineral, and they contain significant amounts of magnesium, phosphorus, and thiamine. They are also rich in protein and dietary fiber.

Chocolate & Brazil Nut Bars

Makes: 9 bars | Prep: 20 minutes, plus 30 minutes chilling | Cook: 4 minutes

Per serving: 334 CAL | 31.5G FAT | 9.6G SAT FAT | 9.9G CARBS | 3.0G SUGAR | 4.1G FIBER | 7.8G PROTEIN | 80MG SODIUM

These bars are ideal for anyone with a sweet tooth, even though they have no sugar. They have a crunchy, chewy texture and are perfect for when out and about.

Ingredients

1 cup slivered almonds

1 cup Brazil nuts, coarsely chopped

5 tablespoons unsalted butter

¼ cup almond butter

1 teaspoon vanilla extract

⅓ cup ground almonds (almond meal)

⅓ cup dry unsweetened coconut

1½ tablespoons rice malt syrup

2 teaspoons cocoa powder

¾ ounce bittersweet chocolate, cut into small chunks

sea salt, to taste (optional)

1. Line a 7½-inch square cake pan with parchment paper. Toast the slivered almonds and Brazil nuts in a dry skillet over high heat until they are light brown, then transfer to a large mixing bowl.

2. Melt the butters together in a small saucepan over low heat. Stir in the vanilla and a pinch of salt, if using.

3. Add all the remaining ingredients to the toasted nuts, then stir. Add the melted butter mixture and stir again. Transfer the batter to the prepared pan and, using the back of a spoon, spread it out to reach all the corners. Cover and chill in the refrigerator for 30 minutes, or until set.

4. Cut into nine bars and wrap each in parchment paper. Store in an airtight container in the refrigerator for up to two days.

Frozen Yogurt-Coated Berries

Serves: 4 | Prep: 20–25 minutes, plus freezing | Cook: none

Per serving : 81 CAL | 0.3G FAT | TRACE SAT FAT | 14.5G CARBS | 10.8G SUGAR | 2.7G FIBER | 6.4G PROTEIN | TRACE SODIUM

These may look like candies, but they are bursting with fruity freshness, vitamin C, and calcium. Keep a handy supply in the freezer.

Ingredients

1 cup fat-free Greek-style yogurt

1 tablespoon honey

¼ teaspoon natural vanilla extract

¾ cup blueberries

1 cup raspberries

1. Line three baking sheets or trays with nonstick parchment paper, checking first that they will fit into your freezer.

2. Put the yogurt, honey, and vanilla extract into a medium bowl and stir together. Drop a few blueberries into the yogurt, then use two forks to coat the berries in a thin layer of yogurt. Lift out, one berry at a time, draining off the excess yogurt, and transfer to one of the lined baking sheets.

3. Continue dipping and coating until all the blueberries are on the baking sheet. Repeat with the raspberries. Freeze, uncovered, for 2–3 hours, until frozen hard.

4. Lift the berries from the baking sheets, then pack into plastic food bags or plastic containers and seal. Freeze for up to one month.

5. Remove as many as you need from the freezer and let thaw for 10 minutes before serving so that the fruit can soften slightly.

Probiotic Prize

Many yogurts are made using active, good bacteria, described as "probiotic." These good bacteria adjust the microflora (the natural balance of organisms) in the intestines, directly benefiting bodily functions, such as digestion and immune function.

Acai

Native to South America, the acai berry,
or palm berry, has strong antioxidant
properties. Produced from the original
berry, using freeze-drying to preserve the
active components, the powder is rich in
dietary fiber, calcium, iron, and vitamin E.
Acai is also rich in B vitamins, electrolytes,
and trace minerals that help reduce
inflammation and improve energy levels.

Fruit & Almond Milk Power Bowl

Serves: 4 | Prep: 15 minutes, plus 8 hours soaking | Cook: none

Per serving: 584 CAL | 17.7G FAT | 3.9G SAT FAT | 97.2G CARBS | 41.8G SUGAR | 14.4G FIBER | 14.8G PROTEIN | 80MG SODIUM

Soaking muesli overnight helps start the breaking down process, making it easier for you to digest. Oats are rich in fiber and good for lasting energy. Choose fruits that are in season—these will be better in flavor and richer in nutrients.

Ingredients

2¾ cups rolled oats

⅓ cup raisins

⅓ cup chopped dried apricots

⅔ cup slivered almonds

2 crisp, sweet apples, grated

2½ cups almond milk

¼ cup Greek-style yogurt

½ cup raspberries

⅓ cup hulled strawberries

⅓ cup blueberries

¼ cup maple syrup

2 tablespoons cacao nibs

1. Mix together the oats, raisins, apricots, almonds, and apples in a large bowl. Pour the milk into the bowl and mix well. Let soak overnight.

2. Divide among four bowls and top each portion with a dollop of yogurt, some raspberries, strawberries, and blueberries, a drizzle of maple syrup, and a sprinkling of cacao nibs.

Why Not Try?

For an easy version, you can soak the muesli overnight, then just top it with fresh fruit in the morning.

Acai Power Bowl

Serves: 4 | Prep: 8 minutes, plus 2 hours freezing | Cook: 8–10 minutes

Per serving : 279 CAL | 4.5G FAT | 0.9G SAT FAT | 58G CARBS | 25.9G SUGAR | 10.1G FIBER | 5.6G PROTEIN | TRACE SODIUM

This is a great way to make quick, healthy dairy-free ice cream without the fuss of an ice cream maker. You could even eat it for breakfast, it's so healthy. Acai berries are high in vitamin A, calcium, fiber, and iron and are thought to be healthy for the blood.

Ingredients

2 bananas, sliced

2⅓ cups raspberries

1 cup rolled oats

2 tablespoons dried cranberries

1 tablespoon sunflower seeds

3 tablespoons maple syrup

⅓ cup soy, almond, rice, or other nondairy milk

1 tablespoon acai powder

⅔ cup blueberries

1. Put the banana slices and 1⅔ cups of the raspberries in a single layer on a baking sheet or tray and freeze for at least 2 hours.

2. Preheat the broiler to medium–hot. Mix together the oats, cranberries, sunflower seeds, and maple syrup and spread over a baking sheet.

3. Cook under the broiler for 8–10 minutes, turning frequently, until golden (watch them carefully, because they can suddenly burn). Let cool.

4. Meanwhile, put half the frozen banana into a food processor with half the frozen raspberries and half the milk. Process until broken down. With the machine running slowly, add the acai powder and the remaining banana, raspberries, and milk, adding enough milk to produce an ice cream consistency.

5. Divide the ice cream among four bowls, top with the blueberries, and sprinkle with the maple-toasted oats.

Spiced Pear & Golden Raisin Strudel

Serves: 6 | Prep: 35 minutes | Cook: 25–30 minutes

Per serving : 448 CAL | 19.1G FAT | 8.6G SAT FAT | 66G CARBS | 29.8G SUGAR | 5.3G FIBER | 6.7G PROTEIN | 80MG SODIUM

This dish is overflowing with fruits, such as pears, golden raisins, and a sprinkling of lemon zest, combined with a little sugar to create a dessert that will wow your friends—and still keep health safely on the culinary agenda.

Ingredients

3 firm, ripe pears, such as Bosc, peeled, cored, and diced

juice and finely grated zest of ½ lemon

⅓ cup raw brown sugar

1 teaspoon ground allspice

⅓ cup golden raisins

½ cup ground almonds

6 sheets phyllo pastry

6 tablespoons unsalted butter, melted, plus extra for greasing

4 teaspoons confectioners' sugar, for dusting

1. Preheat the oven to 400 °F and grease a baking sheet.

2. Mix together the pears, lemon juice and zest, raw sugar, allspice, golden raisins, and half the ground almonds.

3. Place two sheets of phyllo pastry, slightly overlapping, on a clean dish towel. Brush lightly with melted butter and sprinkle with one-third of the remaining ground almonds. Top with two more sheets of phyllo, more melted butter, and half the remaining ground almonds. Repeat once again.

4. Spread the pear mixture along one side, to within 1 inch of the edge. Roll the pastry over to enclose the filling and roll up, using the dish towel to lift. Transfer to the prepared baking sheet and tuck the ends under.

5. Brush the strudel with the remaining melted butter and bake in the preheated oven for 20–25 minutes, until golden and crisp. Serve warm or cold, dusted with confectioners' sugar.

Pear Power

Pears—known to be hypoallergenic—are antibacterial, high in fiber, and contain antioxidants to help prevent cancer and gastroenteritis. They contain a range of nutrients, including vitamin C and potassium, and a good amount of fiber, which helps maintain a healthy colon.

Amaranth & Berry Dessert

Serves: 4 | Prep: 10 minutes, plus soaking & chilling | Cook: 20 minutes, plus standing

Per serving : 217 CAL | 4.1G FAT | 1.8G SAT FAT | 41.4G CARBS | 26.6G SUGAR | 4.3G FIBER | 4.1G PROTEIN | TRACE SODIUM

The grain amaranth is higher in minerals, such as calcium, iron, phosphorous and carotenoids, than most vegetables. Combined with a mixture of berries, loaded with fiber and antioxidants, this delicious dessert will be an all-round success.

Ingredients

½ cup amaranth, soaked overnight

1 cup water

3 cups frozen mixed berries, such as blackberries, blueberries, raspberries, and hulled strawberries, thawed

⅓ cup sugar, or to taste

lemon juice, to taste

1½ tablespoons heavy cream, whipped, to serve

1. Drain the amaranth through a fine strainer, then put it into a saucepan with the water. Bring to a boil, then cover and simmer over low heat for 15 minutes. Remove from the heat, but keep the pan covered for an additional 10 minutes to let the grains swell.

2. Meanwhile, put the berries and sugar into a saucepan, heat over medium heat until almost boiling, then reduce the heat to low and simmer for 3–4 minutes, until soft.

3. Set aside half the berries. Put the remainder into a blender and puree until smooth.

4. Stir the puree into the amaranth along with the lemon juice. Cover and chill in the refrigerator for 1 hour.

5. Divide the mixture among four bowls. Stir in the reserved berries, top each bowl with a spoonful of cream, and serve immediately.

Spicy Cacao & Avocado Mousse

Serves: 4 | Prep: 4 ½ minutes, plus 4 hours chilling | Cook: none

Per serving : 249 CAL | 15.8G FAT | 5.1G SAT FAT | 32.9G CARBS | 17G SUGAR | 11.7G FIBER | 4.9G PROTEIN | TRACE SODIUM

Here's an unusual dessert that you definitely do not have to feel guilty about enjoying—it is full of healthy ingredients and sweetened with agave nectar instead of sugar.

Ingredients

2 ripe avocados, halved and pitted

⅔ cup cacao powder

¼ cup agave nectar

seeds from ½ vanilla bean

½ teaspoon chili powder

¼ cup coconut milk

¼ cup hulled wild or small strawberries

⅓ cup fresh raspberries

½ teaspoon ground cinnamon

1. Scoop the avocado flesh into a large bowl and mash lightly with fork. Stir in the cacao powder, agave nectar, vanilla seeds, and chili powder. Blend thoroughly with a handheld blender until the mixture is thick and smooth. Stir in the coconut milk and blend again.

2. Spoon the avocado mixture into ramekins (individual ceramic dishes) or small, stemmed glasses. Cover with plastic wrap and chill for at least 4 hours.

3. Decorate the avocado mousses evenly with the berries and sprinkle the cinnamon over each dish. Serve immediately.

Cacao Richness

Cacao is rich in antioxidants,
including flavonoids and catechins—
its antioxidant level is higher even
than green and black tea, and cacao is
also packed with fiber.

Mixed Fruit Soup Bowl

Serves: 4 | Prep: 15 minutes, plus 20 minutes chilling | Cook: none

Per serving : 173 CAL | 0.9G FAT | 0.2G SAT FAT | 43.1G CARBS | 34.4G SUGAR | 5.7G FIBER | 2.2G PROTEIN | 40MG SODIUM

This summery cold fruit soup is perfect for a hot day, and it is rich in antioxidants due to its beautiful bright colors. Papaya is also a rich source of proteolytic enzymes, mainly papain, which greatly aid the digestive process. Papain is the most effective enzyme for breaking down meat and other proteins.

Ingredients

2 papayas, peeled, seeded, and chopped

2 cups hulled strawberries

1 honeydew melon, peeled, seeded, and chopped

small handful of fresh mint leaves

1 tablespoon preserved ginger syrup

1 knob preserved ginger

⅔ cup blueberries

1. Reserving 1 tablespoon of the chopped papaya, place the remainder in a food processor with 1¾ cups of the strawberries and process to a smooth puree.

2. Pour into a small bowl and chill in the refrigerator for 10 minutes.

3. Put all but 1 tablespoon of the chopped melon into the food processor with half the mint leaves, the ginger syrup, and preserved ginger. Process to a smooth puree. Pour into a small bowl and chill in the refrigerator for 10 minutes.

4. When you are ready to serve, divide each soup among four bowls, then use a knife to swirl them together. Drop a couple of ice cubes into each bowl.

5. Dice the reserved fruits and sprinkle them over the soup, together with the blueberries and remaining mint leaves.

Green Tea Fruit Salad

Serves: 4 | Prep: 15 minutes, plus 1 hour chilling

Per serving: 313 CAL | 4.8G FAT | 0.6G SAT FAT | 70.8G CARBS | 54G SUGAR | 10G FIBER | 5.2G PROTEIN | TRACE SODIUM

The delicate and refreshing taste of green tea works well for a fruit salad mixed with a hint of honey in a syrup and the addition of chopped fresh mint.

Ingredients

2 teaspoons or 2 tea bags green tea

1 cup boiling water

1 tablespoon honey

⅓ small watermelon, seeded, peeled, and cut into cubes

1 large mango, pitted, peeled, and cut into cubes

1 papaya, seeded, peeled, and cut into cubes

2 Bartlett pears, peeled, cored, and cut into cubes

2 kiwis, peeled and cut into cubes

2 tablespoons coarsely chopped fresh mint

seeds of ½ pomegranate

2 tablespoons coarsely chopped pistachio nuts

1. Put the tea into a small bowl or teapot, pour the boiling water over the leaves, and let brew for 3–4 minutes. Strain into a small bowl, stir in the honey, and let cool.

2. Put the watermelon, mango, and papaya into a large serving bowl, then add the pears, kiwis, and mint. Pour over the cooled green tea and stir gently.

3. Cover the fruit salad with plastic wrap and chill in the refrigerator for 1 hour. Stir gently to mix the tea through the fruit.

4. Spoon the fruit salad into four bowls and serve sprinkled with the pomegranate seeds and pistachio nuts.

Go for Green Tea

Green tea is used in traditional Chinese medicine. It contains antioxidants and is thought to have antibacterial and antiviral properties.

Pineapple Power Cheesecake Bowl

Serves: 4 | Prep: 15 minutes, plus 10 minutes chilling | Cook: 2 minutes

Per serving: 411 CAL | 27.6G FAT | 13.8G SAT FAT | 33.6G CARBS | 20G SUGAR | 3.7G FIBER | 9.3G PROTEIN | 0.7G SALT

Adding tofu to the cream cheese increases the protein content and suddenly makes cheesecake healthy. Pineapple is rich in the enzyme bromelain, known for being efficient at breaking down protein, and is also anti-inflammatory.

Ingredients

7 ounces tofu

1 cup cream cheese

2 tablespoons maple syrup

grated zest of 1 orange

2 tablespoons pecans

½ fresh pineapple, peeled, cored, and chopped (about 2 cups prepared)

2 tablespoons dry unsweetened coconut, toasted

2 teaspoons honey, for drizzling

8 sweet oat cakes (available in gourmet stores and online) or oatmeal cookies

1. Place the tofu, cream cheese, and maple syrup into a food processor and process until smooth.

2. Stir in the orange zest and divide the mixture among four small bowls. Chill in the refrigerator for 10 minutes.

3. Dry-fry the pecans, then coarsely chop.

4. Divide the pineapple among the bowls, then sprinkle with the chopped nuts and coconut.

5. Drizzle each bowl with a little honey.

6. Serve each portion with two sweet oat cakes.

Why Not Try?

This cheesecake works with any fruit topping—try chopped strawberries and mint for a summer version, sprinkled with chopped semisweet chocolate for some decadence. For extra energy, stir 1 tablespoon of maca powder into the cheesecake.

Pineapple

Pineapples have long been used as a
medicinal plant. They are a good source of
vitamin C and other vitamins and minerals,
including magnesium. The pineapple
contains a substance known as bromelain,
which eases inflammation associated with
arthritis and joint pain and may also help to
reduce the incidence of blood clots, which
can lead to heart attacks and strokes.

Baked Figs with Gorgonzola

Serves: 4 | Prep: 15 minutes | Cook: 10 minutes

Per serving: 195 CAL | 5.2G FAT | 2.8G SAT FAT | 28G CARBS | 16.1G SUGAR | 4.2G FIBER | 6.9G PROTEIN | 280MG SODIUM

Made with baby figs, just-melting Gorgonzola, delicate wild flower honey, and crunchy multigrain toast, this snack is simply heavenly.

Ingredients

1 multigrain small baguette or other thin French bread, cut into 8 (¾-inch-thick) slices

8 small fresh figs

2 ounces Gorgonzola cheese, rind removed, cut into 8 squares

4 teaspoons wild flower honey, for drizzling

1. Preheat the oven to 350°F. Lightly toast the bread on both sides, then transfer to a small baking sheet.

2. Cut a cross in the top of each fig, lightly press a cube of cheese into each one, then place a fig on top of each slice of toast. Bake in the preheated oven for 5–6 minutes, until the figs are hot and the cheese is just melting.

3. Transfer to a plate, drizzle with honey, and serve immediately.

Pumpkin Pie Smoothie Bowl

Serves: 4 | Prep: 15 minutes | Cook: 12–15 minutes

Per serving: 341 CAL | 14.8G FAT | 7.5G SAT FAT | 41.7G CARBS | 25.7G SUGAR | 3.3G FIBER | 15.7G PROTEIN | 40MG SODIUM

Pumpkin pie is normally full of sugar with a pastry crust, but this great bowl of goodness makes a filling dessert or breakfast. Topped with thick Greek-style yogurt, rich in probiotics, and toasted seeds, it can be served warm or cold.

Ingredients

3½ cups peeled, seeded, and chopped pumpkin or butternut squash

2 bananas, chopped

1 tablespoon coconut oil

½ teaspoon ground cinnamon

3 tablespoons maple syrup

1¾ cups Greek-style yogurt

3 tablespoons pumpkin seeds, toasted

2 tablespoons sesame seeds, toasted

¼ teaspoon freshly grated nutmeg

1. Place the pumpkin into a saucepan with some water, bring to a boil, then simmer for 12–15 minutes, until tender.

2. Drain, return to the pan, and add the bananas, coconut oil, cinnamon, and maple syrup. Mash to a smooth consistency.

3. Divide among four bowls and top each one with a dollop of yogurt.

4. Sprinkle with the pumpkin seeds, sesame seeds, and nutmeg and serve hot or cold.

Roasted Fruit Crisps

Serves: 4 | Prep: 15 minutes | Cook: 35–40 minutes

Per serving : 410 CAL | 22.5G FAT | 13.6G SAT FAT | 50.7G CARBS | 26.7G SUGAR | 9.7G FIBER | 6.4G PROTEIN | TRACE SODIUM

A healthy take on an old favorite—gooey soft fruits, topped with a nutty coconut crumb topping, rich in fiber but also rich in antioxidants due to the colorful fruits. This is also a perfect dessert for anybody avoiding dairy.

Ingredients

4 apricots, pitted and quartered
1 tablespoon sugar
1⅔ cups raspberries
1⅓ cups blackberries
½ cup rolled oats
⅓ cup whole wheat flour
¼ cup pecans
1 tablespoon sesame seeds
¼ cup packed dark brown sugar
¼ cup coconut oil
coconut yogurt, to serve (optional)

1. Preheat the oven to 350°F.

2. Put the apricot quarters into a roasting pan and sprinkle with the sugar.

3. Roast in the preheated oven for 15 minutes.

4. Spoon the apricots into four ovenproof dishes and sprinkle with the remaining fruits.

5. Put the remaining ingredients into a food processor and process until they resemble lumpy bread crumbs.

6. Spoon the crumb topping over the fruit, place the dishes on a baking sheet, and bake in the oven for 20–25 minutes, until golden and bubbling.

Healthy Fruit & Nut Bowl

Serves: 4 | Prep: 15 minutes, plus 10 minutes chilling | Cook: none

Per serving : 294 CAL | 12G FAT | 1.3G SAT FAT | 44.6G CARBS | 29.9G SUGAR | 11.6G FIBER | 7.8G PROTEIN | TRACE SODIUM

If you have a sweet tooth, then you will adore this—despite it being sugar-free. Wonderful chia seeds, which are rich in fiber and omega-3 fats, are great for giving a liquid a preservelike consistency, so make excellent fruit desserts. Including pineapple provides an enzyme called bromelain, which aids digestion.

Ingredients

1 orange

2 mangoes, peeled, pitted, and chopped

¼ cup chia seeds

¼–⅓ cup milk

2 tablespoons goji berries

seeds from 2 passion fruit

⅓ cup pineapple chunks

2 tablespoons sunflower seeds

2 tablespoons pumpkin seeds, toasted

⅓ cup red currants or blueberries

2 kiwis, peeled and sliced

2 tablespoons slivered almonds, toasted

1. Grate the orange zest, then peel the orange and put the flesh into a food processor with the chopped mango. Process for a few seconds to break everything down.

2. Add the orange zest, chia seeds, and milk and process again for 20–30 seconds, scraping down any mixture from the side of the bowl. Let stand for 5 minutes.

3. Process the mixture again, then divide it among four bowls and chill in the refrigerator for 10 minutes.

4. Top with the remaining ingredients and serve.

Index